All Wrapped Up

All WrappedUp

PITAS, FAJITAS, AND OTHER

SWEET AND SAVORY ROLL UPS

Ellen Brown

BROADWAY BOOKS NEW YORK

BROADWAY

Broadway Books titles may be purchased for business or promotional use or for special sales. For information, please write to: Special Markets Department, Bantam Doubleday Dell Publishing Group, Inc., 1540 Broadway, New York, NY 10036.

BROADWAY BOOKS and its logo, a letter B bisected on the diagonal, are trademarks of Broadway Books, a division of Bantam Doubleday Dell Publishing Group, Inc.

Library of Congress Cataloging-in-Publication Data
Brown, Ellen.
All wrapped up / pitas, fajitas, and other sweet and savory roll ups / Ellen Brown.
— 1st ed.
        p.   cm.
Includes index.
ISBN 0-7679-0137-1
    1. Stuffed foods (Cookery).   2. Cookery, International.   I. Title.   II. Title: Wrap and roll.
TX836.B76   1998
641.8—DC21   97-36111
                                                                              CIP

FIRST EDITION

Designed by Ellen Cipriano

98 99 00 01 02 10 9 8 7 6 5 4 3

Contents

Introduction

I wonder how an ancient Armenian shepherd would feel if he knew that his lavash—a simple flatbread baked on hot stones—is now used as a wrapper in America. Or if any Mexican peasant could ever imagine that flour tortillas would ever be used to enclose everything from savory smoked salmon with herbed cream cheese to the bright crunchy filling of a Chinese egg roll.

In the past few years, wraps have begun to sandbag sandwiches in popularity, appearing on menus of fast-food giants as well as upscale, white tablecloth establishments; wraps are our latest fast-food trend. They have moved beyond the traditional burrito to include any dish that can be stuffed in a pita, rolled in a tortilla, or cupped in a lettuce leaf.

In *All Wrapped Up* you will see how easy it is to create delicious wraps in just minutes in your own kitchen. Many of these recipes merely require assembling or augmenting purchased ingredients, and you can create a meal in far less time than it takes to drive to a fast-food outlet or to have a pizza delivered.

Each recipe calls for 10 or fewer ingredients. In every case, the amount of attended time—not time for marinating or baking when you do not have to be in the kitchen—needed to create the wraps is less than 20 minutes, often no more than 10.

The way that complex and tantalizing taste can be created in such a short amount of time, and with so few ingredients, results from the cornucopia of products now available in supermarkets, such as fresh tomato salsa and prepared pesto sauce. While recipes for creating these foods exist in hundreds of cookbooks, the ones in *All Wrapped Up* were developed using what can be found already prepared.

Wraps are a food trend that has grown faster than the brushfire of mesquite cooking so popular in the late 1980s, and the nontraditional toppings for pizza that followed.

A number of factors go into what differentiates a valid food trend from a fad, and these have contributed to the solid position of wraps on the culinary scene.

First, the wrappers themselves are widely available, versatile, and inexpensive. Pita bread, flour tortillas, and white bread can be found in every establishment selling food in the United States. Armenian lavash and rice paper pancakes can be purchased in many specialty food stores and ethnic markets, and are on their way to national distribution as Middle Eastern and Asian cuisines continue to grow in popularity.

Second, wraps help fill the growing need for food that can be eaten on the run or while driving; wraps are a sit-down meal that can be eaten standing up. As time becomes an increasingly precious commodity, the need for food requiring no utensils has been augmented with the need for food that can be eaten without a plate, and wraps enclose fillings more securely than when fillings are layered "between the bread." You can commute to work eating a nutritious brunch wrap, or munch lunch while walking around town on errands. Wraps are the ultimate in portable meals.

Third, their portability and ease of eating have carved out a niche for wraps in today's style of casual entertaining. Place platters of wraps on a buffet table, or pair platters of fillings with a basket of wraps so that guests can have fun wrapping and rolling.

While the foods used today as wraps have been around for centuries, it is only in the past few decades that their ethnic origins have become popular. Until the mid-1980s, for example, regional American foods were rarely enjoyed outside their ZIP codes of origin. One ate tacos in Tucson, and not in Tampa. Then came the rise in popularity of regional American cooking, as well as the establishment of national chains, which created an increased awareness of such regional specialties as tortillas, and supermarkets began to carry them.

Wraps are a good way to stretch leftovers and transform a "rerun dinner" into an easy meal that is exciting to eat. Many of the recipes in the "Express Lane Wraps" chapter specify foods such as roasted chicken or sliced roast beef that can be purchased in the supermarket. However, homemade tastes best.

Consider the recipes in *All Wrapped Up* as mere guidelines to turning a medley of ingredients into many varied and delicious dishes. Then personalize the recipes to suit your own taste or to make use of ingredients available in your market or kitchen.

Basics for Wrapping

Few experiences are as frustrating as wanting to make a recipe that excites you only to discover that key ingredients cannot be found in your supermarket. Fear not with the recipes in *All Wrapped Up*. They were developed on Nantucket Island during the winter months, when the grocery store inventory is almost as barren as the landscape. Many of the wrappers used can even be found in convenience stores, and by stocking the refrigerator and pantry closet with certain staples, most of these recipes can be created with a moment's notice.

THE WRAPPERS

Here is an introduction to the wrappers used in this book, and how to treat them prior to wrapping:

Flour tortillas: Tortillas come in 6-, 8-, and 10-inch sizes; the two smaller sizes usually come in packs of ten, and the large or "burrito size" is sold eight to a package. Which size to use is specified in each recipe, but feel free to scale the amount up or down. A recipe that creates six servings in a 6-inch tortilla will create four servings if wrapped in the 8-inch tortilla or three servings in the 10-inch size.

   The only trick to handling flour tortillas is to heat them so they can be separated without tearing apart and will be pliable to wrap around the filling. The easiest way is to leave them right in the plastic bag, and microwave on HIGH (100%) for 30 to 45 seconds. If not using an entire package, return the unused tortillas to the refrigerator after tightly sealing the bag.

Alternatively, wrap the tortillas in a tea towel and steam them in a colander for 3 to 4 minutes, or pat them with damp hands and place them in a dry skillet set over medium heat for 30 seconds a side, turning them gently with tongs.

Pristine and white is not the sign of a great tortilla, since they are cooked on a hot griddle. Look for brands that show some brown spots on the surface, as they usually have a more toasted flavor.

Corn tortillas come in the same sizes, however they are not as "wrap-friendly" as flour tortillas. Unless fried in oil, once wrapped around a filling they tend to fall apart. For wraps with southwestern flavors, corn tortillas can be substituted. Use the same size corn tortilla suggested for flour tortillas, and soften the tortillas first using one of the methods specified above.

Pita bread: This Middle Eastern round bread forms a natural pocket when baked. While pitas now come in a few sizes, these recipes were developed using standard 6-inch pitas. For larger portions, 8-inch rounds serve four, or when cut in half, they make eight servings.

While some purists painstakingly separate the sides of the pita by cutting along the edge of the circle and prying the two sides apart, I cut off the top inch.

Most pitas have a thinner and thicker side once opened. When preparing a pita wrap, I indicate whether to start the layering on the thick or thin side. Many recipes simple state "stuff the pita," while others specify to fill the loaves horizontally. This approach is for dishes that combine a thick filling with rice or pasta, and the object is to get some of each with every bite.

Armenian lavash: Some brands of this ancient Armenian flatbread are called "mountain bread" or "shepherd's bread" in supermarkets. Unlike flour tortillas, which they most closely resemble, they have no uniform size, shape, or even texture. Some are round, but large rectangles seem to be the most readily available. In most American supermarkets, what is sold as lavash is a flatbread that is thicker than a tortilla but thinner and more pliable than a pita bread, and an irregular-shaped 18-inch oval. The recipes are calculated on each of these loaves creating two wraps.

True lavash is a large crisp cracker, similar to a matzo, which must be sprinkled with water to soften it to a pliable state before using it as a wrapper. These breads should not be confused with a sesame seed–encrusted cracker sold under the brand name Hawaiian Lavosh.

Depending on their moisture content, which varies from brand to brand, some advance preparation is needed before wrapping or rolling them. If the Armenian lavash seems brittle, soften it by sprinkling it with water, wrap it in plastic wrap, and microwave on HIGH (100%) for 30 seconds. If the lavash is supple, wrap and roll directly from the refrigerator.

Rice paper pancakes: While some supermarkets now stock them, they are most often found in any Asian grocery store or, in a pinch, can be purchased from Asian restaurants. These dried sheets with a lattice-work pattern are sometimes called *galettes de riz* or *banh trang.* Used extensively in Vietnamese cooking, they must be stored in airtight plastic bags or the edges will very quickly curl from contact with moisture in the air.

While wrapping foods in the pancakes requires some fast timing and gentle handling, once you've worked with them a few times this becomes second nature. To soften the sheets, immerse them in a bowl of hot water, and then roll them in a damp towel. Recipes using rice paper pancakes are wrapped just prior to serving if the pancakes are to be served cold, or they can be rolled and baked in advance.

While rice paper pancakes do come in 6- and 12-inch sizes, the most commonly available are 8-inch rounds, which are used in this book. They are sold by weight rather than by count; there are usually about thirty in a 12-ounce package.

Lettuce leaves: Since I'm on a perpetual diet I frequently use lettuce leaves as wrappers, saving my carbo-calories for another meal. I have not, however, imposed my restraint on these recipes, and those dishes specifying lettuce are primarily Asian-inspired. While most supermarkets do not stock Asian varieties of lettuce, both Boston and iceberg lettuce create perfect "cups" for enclosing fillings. Boston lettuce leaves are more pliable than those of crispy iceberg, and do not have a tendency to split apart as easily.

To prepare the leaves as wrappers, cut the core out of the lettuce using a sharp paring knife, and then separate the individual leaves, beginning at the cored end. Rinse them well, and then cut out a V-shape from the core side of the leaves to make them more pliable before rolling. How many packets are needed to create six servings depends on the size of the leaf.

Packaged sandwich bread: Found on the shelf of every grocery store in America, these loaves make a great wrap with very little preparation. Since the crusts are trimmed, it is better to buy uniformly square sandwich bread rather than irregular-shaped loaves.

To prepare the slices, use a serrated bread knife and trim the crusts from a stack of 4 or 5 slices. Place 1 slice at a time on a counter or cutting board, and roll it with a rolling pin, or a wine or soda bottle, until it is flat and rectangular. The bread will then be pliable, and not tear when rolled.

Refrigerated doughs: Some recipes in this book call for refrigerated biscuit dough, pizza dough, or pie-crust sheets. While the tubed doughs can be used directly from the refrigerator, pie-crust sheets should be softened to room temperature, since they are rolled into larger circles. Rather than waiting for the crusts to reach room temperature, you can microwave them on HIGH (100%) for 30 seconds, still wrapped in their plastic envelopes. Use these doughs as specified in the individual recipe.

The Wrap Pantry

In addition to stocking a wrap supply, foods found in the refrigerated case and on supermarket shelves are used for many of these recipes, or you can use them to create your own variations. Here is a basic inventory.

pesto ◎ sun-dried tomato pesto ◎ hummus ◎ barbecue sauce ◎ marinara sauce ◎ mayonnaise ◎ sour cream ◎ plain yogurt ◎ cream cheese ◎ Dijon mustard ◎ ketchup ◎ tomato salsa ◎ canned tomatoes ◎ tomato sauce ◎ long-grain rice ◎ jasmine rice ◎ basmati rice ◎ yellow rice mix ◎ Mexican rice mix ◎ angel hair pasta ◎ vegetable oil spray ◎ olive oil ◎ sesame oil ◎ soy sauce ◎ Thai or Vietnamese fish sauce ◎ oyster sauce ◎ hoisin sauce ◎ chile paste with garlic ◎ pimiento-stuffed green olives ◎ jarred roasted red peppers and/or pimiento strips ◎ canned tuna ◎ canned beans ◎ rice wine vinegar ◎ distilled vinegar ◎ red or white wine vinegar ◎ Cheddar ◎ Monterey and Jalapeño Jack ◎ mozzarella ◎ provolone ◎ Italian Fontina

With these ingredients on hand, you can create an endless variety of wraps. A simple guide to what sauce wraps well is its thickness. While some recipes specify vinaigrette dressings, most wraps are created with spreadable sauces. A few recipes specify yogurt cheese as an ingredient, which is nothing more than yogurt drained of some of its liquid. Place the plain yogurt in a very fine sieve, and suspend the sieve over a mixing bowl. Refrigerate for 4 to 6 hours, or until you can shake it gently and no more liquid drains. The longer the yogurt drains, the thicker it will become.

Time-Saving Tips for Fast Wrapping, Rolling, and Cleanup

Except for dishes wrapped in rice paper pancakes, which must be done one at a time, you can roll foods fastest by using an assembly-line method. It's much faster to pick up a bowl containing a component of the dish once, and spoon some onto each wrapper, than to pick up a few bowls a number of times.

For wraps that are rolled, such as burritos, or to serve wraps without any further cooking, spread them out in front of you on a counter. Proceed to fill the wraps as specified in each recipe, then roll them in succession.

For quesadillas, the filled tortillas should be handled as little as possible to keep the filling from spilling out. The easiest method is to place the tortillas half on a baking sheet covered with heavy-duty aluminum foil and sprayed with vegetable oil spray. Layer the filling on the half of the tortilla that is on the baking sheet, then fold the untreated half of the tortilla over the filling, pressing the quesadillas closed gently with the palm of your hand or a metal spatula. That way the filled quesadillas can be moved around on the baking sheet to space them evenly, and they do not have to be lifted. Then spray the tops with vegetable oil spray, and bake.

If using 6-inch tortillas, six will fit comfortably on one baking sheet; for 8- or 10-inch tortillas use two baking sheets.

The instruction to cover or line pans with heavy-duty foil appears in every appropriate recipe, and that's because scrubbing baked-on cheese off a baking sheet or browned cooking juices from a roasting pan is a needless expense of time and energy. It seems to me that if a dish takes only 10 minutes to prepare, the cleanup should take 1 minute or less.

Another time-saving tip is in the actual preparation of fillings. If at all possible, use a food processor to chop and slice ingredients. Where appropriate, I have indicated in what order to add ingredients to the work bowl, and how to process after the addition of ingredients.

Here is my grand design for using the food processor so that all that's necessary between steps is to rinse it out: Chop the ingredients in order of how messy they are, or how one flavor will impact on that of the next ingredient.

© Using the first approach, the garlic, onions, and bell peppers for a recipe can be chopped in any order, and then placed in separate bowls. You can then end by grating cheese or chopping meat. ◉ Using the second approach, slice apples or chop nuts before chopping onions or garlic.

Turning Individual Wraps Into Appetizers

Wraps, by nature, are great party food, since they are hand-holdable, and by slightly altering some recipes, any wrap in this book can be transformed into an appetizer for a party.

Almost all the quesadilla recipes use 6-inch tortillas, and cutting them in half creates a large solid wedge that enables you to hand-hold it without fear of the filling escaping.

Any individual wrap that can be neatly sliced, such as Pork Satay with Peanut Sauce or Smoked Salmon and Herbed Cream Cheese Roll Ups, are best made with 10-inch flour tortillas rather than smaller ones. Once rolled, they can be sliced into 1-inch sections and presented on a large platter.

For other wraps, roll the filling in the smallest wrapper possible then cut the wrap in half on the diagonal for a pretty presentation that shows the filling. Any dish calling for an Armenian lavash or large flour tortilla can be wrapped in 6-inch sections.

If using pita bread, there are miniature 4-inch versions available in most markets. These should be cut in half and each half should be filled.

One general guideline is don't be overly generous with the fillings if food is to be eaten standing up. Even though it's hand-holdable, an overstuffed pita or half a tortilla roll can still present problems.

Express Lane Wraps

G rab a small basket at the supermarket door, head for the ten items or less lane, and within minutes of getting home you can wrap and roll.

With the exception of occasionally having to boil an egg or fry some bacon, these wraps combine ready-made ingredients in innovative ways. If you're like me, you will have many of these ingredients already on hand.

The supermarket deli department is the source for the cold cuts needed to create, for example, Antipasto Wrap with Italian sausages and vegetables or Roast Beef with Potato Salad.

Other recipes entail purchasing cooked shrimp, already roasted chickens, and other foods that are now supermarket staples. You can also find many excellent fresh bottled salsas in the market. Then there are recipes that call for ingredients from a well-stocked pantry shelf. White Bean and Tuna Salad is created in minutes with canned beans and tuna fish, enlivened with zesty lemon juice and chopped scallion.

Feel free to make substitutions for the meat, fish, or poultry in these recipes, either to use up leftovers or because you prefer another taste or texture.

While no recipe lists more than ten ingredients, the total time involved in producing the dishes is no more than 10 minutes.

Easy White Bread Wraps

As hemlines rise and fall, so does food follow fashion. Here's my nomination for a "retro food" revived from the past—small bread rolls. Back in the sixties, they were all the rage, and why not? They are easy to make, and can be filled with hundreds of options. While a few specific recipes follow, here are two methods for making these food classics. *Serves as many as you like; there are about 18 slices to a 1-pound loaf of white bread*

**Slices of old-fashioned white bread;
purchase a loaf that is as square as
possible to minimize wastage**

1. Trim the crusts from the bread slices, a few slices at a time, using a serrated bread knife. Roll out the slices with a rolling pin or a smooth-sided wine or soda bottle. Place 1 sheet of bread at a time on a flat surface, and roll firmly back and forth using even pressure until the bread slice is flat but still pliable and rectangular. There are two ways of using the bread as a wrapper. The first method creates a swirled pinwheel effect when sliced, and the second makes the bread into a shell to encase the filling. Make pinwheels when the bread is spread with just one or two very thin fillings of a contrasting color, and make rolls when the filling ingredients are thicker.

2. To make pinwheels: Spread a thin layer of the desired fillings or combination of fillings on the entire surface of the bread. If using more than one filling, the layers should be very thin and the firmer spread should be applied first. If using a spread and very thinly sliced meat, poultry, or fish, apply the spread first and top with the solid ingredient. Start at one long side of the bread, and roll up firmly. Repeat with the remaining slices of white bread. Trim the sides of the rolls. Cut into 1- to 1½-inch sections, and arrange on a platter.

3. To make rolls: Place about 1 tablespoon of filling shaped into a log in the center of each bread slice along the long side, and if using a solid ingredient, place it on the center of the spread. You can use anything from asparagus, string beans, and cucumber

Express Lane Wraps 9

to meats and cheeses. Make sure the strips are cut to the length of the bread, and are no more than ⅓ inch in diameter.

Pull the sides of the bread up to enclose the filling, squeezing the edges together gently with your fingers. Place the rolls, seam side down, on a platter and push them gently into a circular shape. Rolls can be cut into thirds or halves, since a smaller section tends to fall apart when picked up.

4. To slice pinwheels or rolls: Both should be sliced with a thin serrated knife very gently using a back-and-forth sawing action. Do not slice directly downward or the bread may collapse.

SUGGESTED FILLINGS FOR PINWHEELS: Smoked salmon and herbed cream cheese (page 123) ◎ cream cheese and sun-dried tomato pesto ◎ honey mustard and very thinly sliced baked ham ◎ basil pesto and very thinly sliced turkey ◎ mayonnaise mixed with very finely chopped shallots and parsley ◎ any sour cream or mayonnaise-based dip found in the supermarket refrigerated case, with thinly sliced meat of your choice ◎ any mayonnaise-based dressing used in recipes later in this chapter

SUGGESTED FILLINGS FOR ROLLS: Hummus with pimiento strips ◎ strawberry cream cheese with strips of mango or papaya ◎ pesto sauce with long strips of provolone

NOTE: Bread rolls are best assembled no more than 3 hours before they are to be served, since the bread absorbs moisture from the fillings. However, the fillings can be prepared in advance and refrigerated, if necessary. Make sure that they reach room temperature and have softened prior to spreading.

Spicy Pacific Rim Shrimp

This easy recipe combines shrimp, orange slices, and crisp vegetables in a spicy, aromatic dressing. It's one of my favorite party dishes, and is great just served as a salad, too. *Serves 6*

SUGGESTED WRAPPERS: Rice paper pancakes ◎ eight-inch flour tortillas

1 to 1½ pounds cooked and peeled
    medium shrimp
½ cup thinly sliced red onion
1 cucumber, peeled, halved, seeded, and
    cut into thin slices
1 navel orange, peeled, halved, and cut
    into thin slices
¼ pound fresh spinach, stemmed,
    rinsed, and thinly sliced

3 tablespoons sesame seeds, toasted
    (optional)
3 tablespoons hoisin sauce
2 tablespoons rice wine vinegar
1 to 2 teaspoons chile paste with garlic
    (see Note)
3 tablespoons vegetable oil
2 tablespoons sesame oil

   1. Combine the shrimp, red onion, cucumber, orange, spinach, and sesame seeds, if used, in a large bowl. Combine the hoisin sauce, vinegar, chile paste, vegetable oil, sesame oil in a jar with a tight-fitting lid, and shake well to combine. Pour the dressing over the salad, and toss well.

   2. Fill a wide mixing bowl with very hot tap water. Place a damp tea towel in front of you on the counter. Place the rice paper pancakes on a plate, and cover with a barely damp towel. Line a baking sheet with plastic wrap.

   3. Fill one rice paper pancake at a time, keeping the remainder covered. Totally immerse the pancake in the hot water for 2 seconds. Remove it and place it on the damp tea towel; it will become pliable within a few seconds. Gently fold the front edge of the pancake ⅓ of the way to the top. Place a portion of salad on the folded-up edge, and shape it into a log, leaving a 1½-inch margin on each side. Fold the sides of the pancake over the filling, and roll tightly but gently, beginning with the filled side. Take a second sheet of rice paper, and soften it. Place the filled roll in the center of the sheet, fold the sides over it, and roll it gently.

4. Place the roll on the baking sheet, and continue to fill the rice paper pancakes in the same manner. Cut each roll in half on the diagonal, and serve immediately.

NOTE: If using flour tortillas, place a portion of salad along one edge, leaving a 1½-inch margin on both sides. Tuck the sides in to enclose the filling, and then wrap it firmly but gently, beginning with the filled side. Cut in half on the diagonal, and serve immediately. Chile paste with garlic is available in most supermarkets, but you can substitute ½ teaspoon Tabasco sauce and 1 garlic clove, peeled and crushed.

Shrimp with Chick Pea and Olive Salad

Chick peas have a delicate flavor and a meaty texture that absorbs the taste of dressings well. Combining them with succulent shrimp and tangy olives creates a wonderful light wrap. *Serves 6*

SUGGESTED WRAPPERS: Pita bread ◉ eight-inch flour tortillas

One 1-pound can chick peas, drained
    and rinsed
½ cup sliced pimiento-stuffed green
    olives
4 scallions, white parts and 4 inches of
    green tops, trimmed and thinly
    sliced
1 pound peeled and deveined cooked
    medium shrimp, about 25

¼ cup white wine vinegar
1 tablespoon minced garlic
1 teaspoon dried Italian seasoning
Salt and freshly ground black pepper
¼ cup extra virgin olive oil
6 romaine or Boston lettuce leaves
3 plum tomatoes, cored, seeded, and
    thinly sliced

1. Place the chick peas, olives, scallions, and shrimp in a mixing bowl. Combine the vinegar, garlic, Italian seasoning, and salt and pepper to taste, in a jar with a tight-fitting lid, and shake well. Add the olive oil, and shake well again to combine. Pour the dressing over the salad, and toss to coat well. Allow the mixture to sit for at least 15 minutes at room temperature; it can be refrigerated, tightly covered with plastic wrap, for up to 1 day.

2. Place a lettuce leaf and some tomato slices on the thin side of each pita pocket, and stuff the salad into the pita. Serve immediately.

NOTE: If using flour tortillas, place a lettuce leaf, tomato slices, and a portion of the salad along one edge, leaving a 2-inch margin on one side. Tuck the end in to enclose the filling, and then roll the tortillas firmly but gently, beginning on the filled side. Serve immediately.

Crab with Crunchy Fennel Salad

Once a cuisine gains popularity, the fresh vegetables that play a role in it are easy to find, and that has been the case with crisp, anise-scented fresh fennel bulbs. Light and refreshing, this salad joins lemony fennel salad with morsels of delectable crab. *Serves 6*

SUGGESTED WRAPPERS: Pita bread ☉ Boston or iceberg lettuce leaves

1 pound lump crabmeat

1 large fennel bulb, cored and very thinly sliced

¼ cup chopped fresh parsley

¼ cup fruity olive oil

3 tablespoons freshly squeezed lemon juice

2 teaspoons anchovy paste (optional)

1 garlic clove, peeled and crushed

Freshly ground black pepper

Salt, if not using anchovy paste

6 romaine or Boston lettuce leaves (omit if wrapping in lettuce cups); see Note

3 plum tomatoes, cored, seeded, and thinly sliced

1. Spread the crab on a plate, carefully pick it over, and discard any bits of shell. Set aside.

2. Combine the fennel and parsley in a large mixing bowl. Combine the olive oil, lemon juice, anchovy paste (or salt), garlic, and pepper to taste in a jar with tight-fitting lid, and shake well to combine. Pour the dressing over the salad, and toss well to coat. Gently fold in the crab.

3. Line the thin side of each pita pocket with a lettuce leaf and some tomato slices. Stuff in a portion of salad, and serve immediately.

NOTE: If using lettuce cups, place a portion of salad in the center of each cup and top with a tomato slice. Fold the sides of the lettuce up around the filling. The salad can be prepared up to 6 hours in advance and refrigerated, tightly covered with plastic wrap. Do not roll until just prior to serving. Diced shrimp can be substituted for the crab.

Club Wrap with Roasted Garlic

Certain sandwich fillings have become favorites since they just plain work, and the club sandwich combo is one of them. Here, the mayonnaise is flavored with heady roasted garlic and the filling is wrapped in a thin tortilla. *Serves 6*

SUGGESTED WRAPPERS: Ten-inch flour tortillas ◎ Armenian lavash

2 to 3 tablespoons roasted garlic puree
    (see Note)
1/2 cup mayonnaise
Salt and freshly ground black pepper
12 romaine or iceberg lettuce leaves,
    shredded

4 plum tomatoes, cored, seeded, and
    thinly sliced
1 1/2 pounds bacon, fried crisp and
    drained on paper towels
1/2 pound thinly sliced chicken or
    smoked chicken

1. Mix the garlic puree into the mayonnaise, and stir well. Season with salt and pepper to taste, and set aside.

2. Place the wrappers on a counter, and spread the garlic mayonnaise on the entire surface of each. Place the shredded lettuce on one edge of the wrapper, leaving a 2-inch margin on one side. Top the lettuce with tomato, bacon, and chicken slices. Spread more mayonnaise on the chicken, and sprinkle the chicken with salt and pepper to taste. Tuck the side of the wrapper over the filling, and then roll the wrapper firmly but gently, beginning with the side layered with the filling. Serve immediately.

NOTE: The garlic mayonnaise can be made up to 3 days in advance and refrigerated. Roasted garlic puree is available in most specialty food stores, but it can be easily made at home. Cut the top ½ inch off a head of garlic, and rub the entire head with olive or vegetable oil. Wrap the garlic head loosely in heavy-duty aluminum foil with the top exposed, and bake it in a preheated 375°F. oven for 45 minutes. When cool enough to handle, separate the garlic cloves and press them from the stem end; the cloves will pop out of their skins. Puree the garlic in a food processor or press it through a potato ricer. The puree can be refrigerated for up to 4 days.

Juicier Lemons

To get more juice from lemons, pierce them a few times with a meat fork or the tip of a sharp knife, and then microwave on HIGH (100%) for 30 seconds.

Shrimp or Crab with Garlicky Italian Vegetables

The aisle in the supermarket containing the Italian pickled vegetables is a treasure trove for making easy and delicious wraps. The bright flavor of pickled vegetables mixed with crunchy celery and delicate shrimp makes this a winner. *Serves 6*

SUGGESTED WRAPPERS: Pita bread ◎ Armenian lavash

1½ pounds cleaned and deveined, cooked medium shrimp or 1 pound lump crabmeat (picked over to remove any fragments of shell)
¾ cup finely diced celery
¾ cup finely chopped pickled Italian giardiniera vegetables
One 4-ounce jar pimiento slices, drained
4 large garlic cloves, peeled and minced
½ cup chopped fresh parsley
2 tablespoons chopped fresh oregano
¼ cup freshly squeezed lemon juice
½ cup extra virgin olive oil
Salt and freshly ground black pepper
6 to 12 romaine or Boston lettuce leaves
3 plum tomatoes, cored, seeded, and thinly sliced

1. Place the shrimp or crab in a large mixing bowl along with the celery, giardiniera vegetables, pimientos, garlic, parsley, and oregano.

2. Combine the lemon juice, olive oil, and salt and pepper to taste in a jar with a tight-fitting lid, and shake well to combine. Pour the dressing over the salad, and toss gently. Allow to sit at room temperature for 15 minutes to blend the flavors.

3. To serve, line the thin side of the pocket of the pita bread with lettuce leaves and insert tomato slices. Spoon the salad into the pocket and serve immediately.

NOTE: If using lavash, place the lettuce leaves and tomato slices along one side, leaving a 2-inch margin. Mound the filling on top, and roll gently but firmly. Both the seafood and vegetable marinade can be prepared up to a day in advance and kept tightly covered in the refrigerator. Do not combine them until a few hours before serving time or the seafood will absorb too much of the marinade flavor.

Harriet's Honeymoon Smoked Salmon Burritos

This dish comes from my friend and editor Harriet Bell, who encountered them on her honeymoon in the Canadian Rockies. The colorful and delicious wraps marry the fresh tastes of cilantro and onion with satiny smoked salmon. *Serves 4 to 6*

SUGGESTED WRAPPERS: Ten-inch flour tortillas ◎ Armenian lavash

¹/₄ cup tightly packed fresh cilantro leaves
1 garlic clove, peeled and sliced
¹/₄ teaspoon chipotle chiles in adobo sauce or Tabasco sauce, or more to taste

¹/₂ cup mayonnaise
¹/₄ pound thinly sliced smoked salmon
¹/₂ small red onion, peeled and thinly sliced
One 4-ounce jar sliced pimientos, drained

1. Place the cilantro, garlic, chipotles, and mayonnaise in the bowl of a food processor fitted with the steel blade or in a blender. Process until well combined but not pureed; there should be flecks of cilantro visible. Scrape the mixture into a covered container, and refrigerate until needed.

2. Place either tortillas or lavash on the kitchen counter. Spread each wrapper with a thin layer of cilantro mayonnaise. Cover the bottom half of each tortilla with slices of salmon and top with onion and sliced pimientos. Roll the tortillas firmly but gently, beginning with the side layered with the filling. Cut the burritos into thirds or halves on the diagonal, and serve immediately.

NOTE: The cilantro mayonnaise can be prepared up to 4 hours in advance and kept refrigerated; however do not assemble the burritos more than 2 hours prior to serving.

Pan Bagnat

Try this wrap variation on the famous French sandwich from sunny Provence. The name comes from *pain baigné,* which means "bathed bread." The combination of crunchy vegetables with mellow tuna and egg is fantastic. Most recipes for *pain baigné* call for the sandwiches to sit for a while to allow the bread to become soaked with dressing. This faster—and neater—version achieves the same objective by breaking bits of pita into the salad dressing. *Serves 6*

6 pita breads
³/₄ cup Caesar salad dressing
Two 7-ounce cans tuna packed in oil, drained, and broken into chunks
3 plum tomatoes, cored, seeded, and thinly sliced
¹/₂ medium cucumber, peeled, halved, seeded, and thinly sliced
¹/₄ cup coarsely chopped red onion

¹/₄ cup pimiento slices
2 large hard-cooked eggs, peeled and sliced
¹/₂ cup pitted and chopped Niçoise, Greek, or Italian olives
1 tablespoon nonpareil capers, drained
¹/₄ cup chopped fresh basil
6 romaine or iceberg lettuce leaves (optional)

1. Cut the top ¹/₃ off each pita bread, and dice the tops into ¹/₄-inch pieces. Place pita bits in a large mixing bowl, and pour the dressing over them, tossing well.

2. Add all the remaining ingredients except the lettuce leaves, if used, to the mixing bowl. Toss gently to combine with the soaked pita pieces. Line the thin side of the pita bread, if desired, with lettuce, and then spoon the salad into the bread. Serve immediately.

NOTE: Most of the salad ingredients can be prepared up to 1 day in advance and refrigerated, tightly covered with plastic wrap. Do not add the onion or basil until just prior to serving.

Smoked Trout and Asparagus Rolls

These make a wonderful appetizer for brunch as well as for a cocktail party. With the green dot of asparagus in the center of the creamy trout mousse dotted with flecks of olive and parsley, these resemble Japanese hand rolls. *Makes 24 to 36 pieces, depending on how they are cut*

½ pound boneless smoked trout fillets,
    skin discarded
2 to 4 tablespoons mayonnaise
1 tablespoon freshly squeezed lemon
    juice
1 tablespoon sour cream or nonfat
    yogurt
Freshly ground black pepper
1 tablespoon fresh parsley leaves,
    washed and dried

¼ cup pimiento-stuffed green olives
12 slices white bread, trimmed and
    rolled flat (page 9)
6 large asparagus stalks, peeled, cooked,
    and chilled
¼ cup finely chopped fresh parsley, for
    garnish (optional)

1. Break up the trout into 2-inch sections, and combine with 2 tablespoons mayonnaise, lemon juice, sour cream, and pepper to taste in a food processor fitted with the steel blade. Puree until smooth, scraping down the sides of the work bowl and adding more mayonnaise to create a mixture with the consistency of softened cream cheese; the amount of mayonnaise needed will depend on the moisture content of the trout.

2. Add the parsley leaves, and pulse to chop finely. Add the olives, and pulse to chop finely. Scrape the mixture into a mixing bowl.

3. Spread 1 tablespoon trout mixture evenly over the rolled bread. Cut a stalk of asparagus in half and place in the center of each bread slice. Bring the edges up to meet. Place rolls, seam side down, on a baking sheet lined with waxed paper or plastic wrap. Repeat with remaining bread slices and asparagus.

4. Cut each roll with a serrated knife. If cut into thirds, stand them upright on a platter to resemble Japanese hand rolls. If cut into halves, place them, seam side down, to resemble small logs. Press ends of rolls gently into finely chopped parsley for garnish, if desired.

NOTE: The trout spread and asparagus can be prepared up to a day in advance and refrigerated, covered with plastic wrap. Do not roll or slice more than 2 hours before serving.

Easy Zesting

If using a box or flat grater with tiny holes, rub the surface of the citrus fruit backward and forward on the grid two or three times to remove the zest without any of the bitter white pith. Place a piece of parchment paper on the grater first, and the zest will stay on the parchment, making it easy to remove.

Italian White Bean and Tuna Salad

White beans and chunks of tuna salad lightly dressed with olive oil and lemon juice is an antipasto I remember from my first trip to Italy as a teenager, and I have been making it ever since. This combination is refreshing when scallion and tangy lemon serve as a foil to the tender beans and tuna. This easy, quick filling is suitable for a variety of wraps. *Serves 6*

SUGGESTED WRAPPERS: Pita bread ◎ eight-inch flour tortillas ◎ Boston or iceberg lettuce leaves

One 19-ounce can white beans, drained and rinsed

Two 6½-ounce cans light tuna packed in olive oil or vegetable oil

⅓ cup finely chopped fresh parsley

1 teaspoon crushed garlic

½ cup finely chopped scallions, white parts and 3 inches of green tops

2 tablespoons freshly squeezed lemon juice

Salt and freshly ground black pepper

6 romaine or Boston lettuce leaves (omit if wrapping in lettuce cups)

3 plum tomatoes, cored, seeded, and thinly sliced

1. Place the beans in a mixing bowl. Break the tuna into chunks, and add it to the beans along with the oil in the can. Mix the remaining salad ingredients together well, and gently fold into the beans and tuna. Season with salt and pepper to taste, and chill for 10 minutes.

2. Line the thin side of the pita pocket with a lettuce leaf and a few tomato slices, and stuff the tuna and bean salad into the pita. Serve immediately.

NOTE: If using flour tortillas, place a lettuce leaf along one edge, leaving a 1½-inch margin on both sides. Top the lettuce with some tomato slices and a portion of salad. Tuck in the sides to enclose the filling, and roll the tortilla firmly but gently, beginning with the filled edge. Cut in half, and serve immediately. If using lettuce cups, place a portion of salad in the center of each, and top with a few tomato slices. The salad can be prepared up to 2 days in advance and refrigerated, tightly covered with plastic wrap. Allow it to reach room temperature before serving.

Pacific Rim Chicken

The dressing for this refreshing filling of crunchy vegetables, delicate chicken, and luscious mango is similar to a chutney, but it needs no cooking. Search out jarred mango slices in the produce section of your supermarket; they are delicious and a much better choice than an unripe mango. *Serves 6*

SUGGESTED WRAPPERS: Rice paper pancakes ◎ eight-inch flour tortillas

2 cups thinly sliced cooked chicken, torn into shreds
1 cup bean sprouts, rinsed
1 cup thinly sliced celery or bok choy
1 carrot, peeled and cut into long slices
1 ripe mango, peeled and cut into ¹/₂-inch dice
¹/₃ cup apricot jam

1 teaspoon grated fresh ginger
¹/₄ cup cider vinegar
¹/₂ teaspoon curry powder
1 teaspoon Worcestershire sauce
¹/₄ teaspoon Tabasco sauce
Salt and freshly ground black pepper

1. Combine the chicken, bean sprouts, celery, carrot, and mango in a mixing bowl.

2. In a small bowl, combine the apricot jam, ginger, vinegar, curry powder, Worcestershire sauce, and Tabasco. Stir well, and season with salt and pepper to taste. Drizzle the sauce over the filling, and toss gently to coat all the ingredients.

3. Fill a wide mixing bowl with very hot tap water. Place a damp tea towel in front of you on the counter. Place the rice paper pancakes on a plate, and cover with a barely damp towel. Line a baking sheet with plastic wrap.

4. Fill one rice paper pancake at a time, keeping the remainder covered. Totally immerse the pancake in the hot water for 2 seconds. Remove it and place it on the damp tea towel; it will become pliable within a few seconds. Gently fold the front edge of the pancake 1/3 of the way to the top. Place a portion of salad on the folded-up edge, and shape it into a log, leaving a 1½-inch margin on each side. Fold the sides over the filling, and roll tightly but gently, beginning with the filled side. Take a second sheet of rice paper, and soften it. Place the filled roll in the center of the sheet, fold the sides over it, and roll it gently.

5. Place the roll on the baking sheet, and continue to fill the rice paper pancakes in the same manner. Cut each roll in half on the diagonal, and serve immediately.

NOTE: If using flour tortillas, place a portion of salad along one edge of each one, leaving a 1½-inch margin on both sides. Tuck the sides in to enclose the filling, and then wrap the tortillas firmly but gently, beginning with the filled side. Cut in half on the diagonal, and serve immediately.

Add Crunch to Wraps

Alfalfa sprouts can be substituted for bean sprouts in salad wraps, but they are far too delicate to cook for even a few minutes. Substitute matchstick-size pieces of bok choy, Napa cabbage, or celery to impart the same crunchy texture and light color of alfalfa sprouts.

Curried Chicken with Grapes and Chutney

One of the first dishes I made for a dinner party as a teenager was curried chicken, accompanied by bowls of grapes, almonds, and other condiments. The assertive flavor of curry is a great way to perk up chicken, and the grapes make this a pretty and delicious wrap. *Serves 6*

SUGGESTED WRAPPERS: Pita bread ◎ eight-inch flour tortillas ◎ Boston or iceberg lettuce leaves

½ cup chutney, such as Major Grey's
¾ cup mayonnaise
1 to 2 tablespoons curry powder
¼ cup sweetened, shredded coconut, toasted
1 pound roasted chicken, diced
½ cup sliced celery

¾ cup halved green or red seedless grapes
½ cup sliced almonds, toasted
Salt and freshly ground black pepper
6 to 12 leaves Boston or romaine lettuce (omit if wrapping in lettuce leaves)

   1. Place the chutney in a food processor fitted with the steel blade, and chop finely using an on-and-off pulsing action. Combine the chutney with the mayonnaise, curry powder, and coconut in a large mixing bowl. Add the chicken, celery, grapes, and almonds to the bowl, and mix gently to combine. Season with salt and pepper to taste.
   2. If using pita bread, line the pocket with lettuce leaves, and stuff in a portion of salad.

NOTE: If wrapping in flour tortillas, place lettuce leaves on one edge of each tortilla, leaving a 1½-inch margin on both sides. Place a portion of filling in an even line on top of the lettuce. Tuck in the sides to enclose the filling, and then roll tightly but gently, beginning with the filled edge. If wrapping in lettuce leaves, place a portion of filling at the stem end of the leaf and roll to the large end, tucking in the sides. The salad can be prepared up to 1 day in advance and refrigerated, tightly covered. If preparing in advance, do not add the almonds until just prior to serving.

Turkey Tonnato Wrap

Vitello tonnato is a classic Italian summer veal dish; turkey breast makes a convenient and equally delicious substitute for the veal. With the addition of salad greens and vegetables, the meal-in-a-wrap is complete. *Serves 6*

SUGGESTED WRAPPERS: Pita bread ◎ eight-inch flour tortillas

One 7-ounce can tuna packed in oil, drained
¹/₂ cup olive oil
¹/₄ cup freshly squeezed lemon juice
2 tablespoons anchovy paste (optional)
1 tablespoon nonpareil capers

Salt and freshly ground black pepper
2 cups mesclun salad, rinsed and dried
1¹/₂ pounds thinly sliced turkey breast
2 jarred roasted red bell peppers, cut into ¹/₂-inch slices
¹/₂ cup sliced pitted green olives

1. Combine the tuna, olive oil, lemon juice, and anchovy paste, if used, in a food processor fitted with the steel blade or in a blender. Puree until smooth, scraping the sides of the bowl as needed. Scrape the sauce into a small mixing bowl, and stir in the capers. Season with salt and pepper to taste; if anchovy paste was used, little, if any, salt will be needed.

2. Spread a thick layer of filling on both sides of the pita pocket, and insert a layer of salad greens. Divide the turkey breast into 6 portions, and spread each with more of the tuna sauce. Place portions of red pepper and olives on top of the tuna sauce, then fold the turkey into packets that will fit into the pitas. Tuck the packets into the pitas, and serve immediately.

NOTE: If using flour tortillas, spread them with tuna sauce, and then place a portion of turkey along one edge, leaving a 1¹/₂-inch margin on both sides. Spread the turkey with more sauce, and then divide the salad greens, red peppers, and olives and place on top. Tuck in the sides, and roll the tortilla firmly but gently around the filling, beginning with the filled edge. The tuna sauce can be made up to 2 days in advance and refrigerated, tightly covered.

Smoked Turkey, Salsa, and Guacamole Roll Ups

These roll ups can be assembled in less time than it takes to wait at the supermarket checkout if you buy prepared guacamole. But by making the guacamole yourself in a plastic bag, there is no cleanup. Crunchy jicama and tangy fresh cilantro adds texture and mild flavor to this dish. *Serves 6*

SUGGESTED WRAPPERS: Eight-inch flour tortillas ◎ Armenian lavash

3 ripe avocados
1/2 small red onion, peeled and finely diced
1 or 2 jalapeño chiles, seeds and ribs removed, finely diced
5 plum tomatoes, cored, seeded, and diced

1/4 cup chopped fresh cilantro leaves
1 tablespoon freshly squeezed lime juice
Salt
1 small jicama
6 large romaine or Boston lettuce leaves
1 1/2 pounds smoked turkey, thinly sliced
1/2 cup tomato salsa

1. Cut the avocados in half, and discard the pits. Spoon the flesh into a heavy resealable plastic bag. Extract as much air as possible from the bag, and close the bag. Mash the avocados by squeezing the bag with your hands, or place the bag on the kitchen counter and mash them with the blunt side of a meat mallet. Open the bag, add the onion, chiles, half the tomatoes, cilantro, lime juice, and salt to taste. Reseal the bag and combine the mixture with your hands. Set aside.

2. Using a sharp paring knife, remove the outer brown peel from the jicama, and then remove the inner fibrous peel. Cut the jicama into 1/2-inch thick slices, and then cut each slice into 1/2-inch strips.

3. Place a lettuce leaf on one edge of each wrapper, leaving a 1 1/2-inch margin on both sides. Place a few slices of turkey on top of the lettuce, and then top the turkey with jicama, the remaining tomatoes, guacamole, and salsa. Repeat the layering with turkey, guacamole, and salsa, then tuck in the sides to enclose the filling, and roll the wrappers firmly but gently, beginning with the filled edge. Cut in half on the diagonal, and serve immediately.

Thanksgiving Wrap

Now you can wrap your way out of those leftover-turkey doldrums. After the stuffing and gravy are gone, and the football games are over, try this. *Serves 6*

SUGGESTED WRAPPERS: Eight-inch flour tortillas ◎ pita bread

One 8-ounce package cream cheese,
    softened
1 tablespoon grated orange zest
3 tablespoons freshly squeezed orange
    juice

$1/2$ cup chopped pecans, toasted
6 romaine or Boston lettuce leaves
$1^1/2$ pounds thinly sliced turkey breast
Salt and freshly ground black pepper
1 cup whole-berry cranberry sauce

1. Combine the cream cheese, zest, and orange juice in a small bowl. Beat with a spoon until well mixed. Stir in the nuts.

2. Place the tortillas on a counter, and spread the cream cheese on the entire surface of each one. Place a lettuce leaf on one edge, leaving a $1^1/2$-inch margin on both sides. Place turkey slices on top of the lettuce, and sprinkle the turkey with salt and pepper to taste. Top the turkey with the cranberry sauce. Tuck the sides in to enclose the filling, and roll the tortillas tightly but gently, beginning with the filled edge. Serve immediately.

NOTE: If using pita bread, spread the cream cheese on both sides of the pocket. Fold a portion of turkey so that it fits into the pocket, and tuck some cranberry sauce into the center of the package. Insert the package into the pita. The cream cheese mixture can be prepared up to 2 days in advance and refrigerated, tightly covered. Bring to room temperature to soften before assembling the wraps.

Smoked Turkey with Chutney Mayonnaise and Toasted Peanuts

The sweet/sour/hot flavors of traditional chutneys add a wonderful flavor to smoked turkey. Peanuts and crunchy vegetables give this wrap some textural interest. *Serves 6*

SUGGESTED WRAPPERS: Eight-inch flour tortillas ◎ Armenian lavash ◎ pita bread

1/2 cup mayonnaise
1/2 cup mango chutney, such as Major Grey's
1/4 cup chopped fresh cilantro leaves
1 cup sliced celery or bok choy
1/2 cup diced red onion
1/2 cup diced red bell pepper

3/4 cup cocktail peanuts (not dry-roasted), toasted and coarsely chopped
Salt and freshly ground black pepper
6 romaine or iceberg lettuce leaves
1 1/2 pounds thinly sliced smoked turkey

1. Combine the mayonnaise and chutney in a food processor fitted with the steel blade or in a blender, and puree until smooth. Stir in the cilantro, and set aside. Combine the celery, onion, red bell pepper, and peanuts, and stir in 2/3 of the mayonnaise mixture.

2. Place the tortillas or lavash on the counter, and place a lettuce leaf on one edge, leaving a 1 1/2-inch margin on both sides. Spread the lettuce with the chutney mayonnaise, and arrange a portion of turkey on top of the lettuce, and sprinkle the turkey with salt and pepper to taste. Mound a portion of salad on top of the turkey, tuck in the sides to enclose the filling, and roll the wrappers firmly but gently, beginning with the filled edge. Cut in half on the diagonal, and serve immediately.

NOTE: If using pita bread, spread some of the chutney mayonnaise inside the pocket, and place a lettuce leaf on the thin side of the pocket. Fold a portion of turkey into a packet that conforms to the shape of the pita. Insert the turkey packets into the pitas, and then stuff in some of the vegetable mixture. Serve immediately. Roast pork or chicken can be substituted for the smoked turkey.

South of the Border Beef

Hearty beef, smoky bacon, and chunky salsa put a southwestern twist on this wrap. The mayonnaise makes the sauce smooth and creamy while the salsa and chiles deliver a powerful punch of flavor. You can tone the heat down or turn it up; it depends on how spicy you like your salsa. *Serves 6*

SUGGESTED WRAPPERS: Eight-inch flour tortillas ◎ pita bread

1/3 cup mayonnaise
1/3 cup refrigerated chunky tomato salsa, drained
One 4-ounce can chopped green chiles, drained (optional)
1/4 cup chopped fresh cilantro leaves
Salt and cayenne pepper

6 to 12 large Boston or romaine lettuce leaves
1 pound rare roast beef, thinly sliced
3 plum tomatoes, cored, seeded, and thinly sliced
12 slices bacon, fried crisp and drained on paper towels

1. In a small bowl, combine the mayonnaise, salsa, chiles, and cilantro. Stir well, season with salt and cayenne to taste, and set aside.

2. Place the tortillas on a counter, and spread a thin layer of salsa mayonnaise over the entire tortilla, and place a lettuce leaf on one edge, leaving a 1½-inch margin on both sides. Place a portion of roast beef on the lettuce, and then spread the roast beef

with another layer of salsa mayonnaise. Place slices of tomato and 2 slices of bacon in the center of each tortilla. Tuck the sides over to enclose the filling, and roll the tortillas firmly but gently, beginning with the filled edge. Cut each roll in half on the diagonal, and serve immediately.

NOTE: If using pita bread, spread a layer of salsa mayonnaise on both sides of the pocket, and insert lettuce. Divide the roast beef into 6 portions, and fold each into a package that will fit in the pita. Place a dollop of salsa mayonnaise in the center of each pocket, and insert some tomato slices and 2 slices of bacon. Tuck the roast beef package into the pita. The salsa mayonnaise can be prepared up to 2 days in advance and refrigerated, tightly covered.

Asian Beef Wrap

This simple wrap is imbued with all the heady flavors and aromas of Asian food, and the crunchy vegetables are a textural contrast to the beef. It's a great way to use up any leftover steak or roast beef, too. *Serves 6*

SUGGESTED WRAPPERS: Ten-inch flour tortillas ◎ Armenian lavash

1 tablespoon Dijon mustard
2 tablespoons hoisin sauce
2 tablespoons soy sauce
Freshly ground black pepper
1/4 cup sesame oil
1/4 cup vegetable oil
1 pound rare roast beef, thinly sliced
1/4 pound snow peas, trimmed, blanched

for 30 seconds, and sliced in half
lengthwise if large
3 cups fresh spinach, stemmed, rinsed,
and dried
1 cup fresh bean sprouts, rinsed
1 red bell pepper, seeds and ribs
removed, thinly sliced

1. Combine the mustard, hoisin sauce, soy sauce, and pepper to taste in a jar with a tight-fitting lid, and shake well. Add the sesame and vegetable oils, and shake again. Set aside.

2. Slice the roast beef into 2-inch strips, and separate the slices. Place the slices in a large mixing bowl, along with the snow peas, spinach, bean sprouts, and red bell pepper. Pour the dressing over the salad, and toss well to coat all ingredients.

3. Place the wrappers on a counter, and place a portion of salad on one edge, leaving a 2-inch margin on both sides. Tuck the sides over to enclose the filling, and roll the wrappers firmly but gently, beginning with the filled edge. Cut in half on the diagonal, and serve immediately.

NOTE: The salad can be prepared up to 3 hours in advance and refrigerated, tightly covered.

Roast Beef with Potato Salad

This hearty and satisfying meal-in-a-wrap is a classic meat and potatoes combination that is completely portable. Using potato salad from the deli case that has been perked up with parsley, onion, and pickle, this wrap can be assembled in minutes. *Serves 6*

SUGGESTED WRAPPERS: Ten-inch flour tortillas ◎ pita bread

1 pound potato salad in vinaigrette
   dressing, not mayonnaise
1/4 cup chopped fresh parsley
1/2 cup diced red onion
1 large dill pickle, coarsely chopped

Salt and freshly ground black pepper
6 romaine or iceberg lettuce leaves
1 pound rare roast beef, thinly sliced
3 plum tomatoes, cored, seeded, and
   sliced

1. Combine the potato salad, parsley, onion, and pickle in a mixing bowl, and mix well. Season with salt and pepper to taste, and set aside.

2. Place the tortillas on a counter, and place 1 lettuce leaf along the edge of each, leaving a 2-inch margin on both sides. Top the lettuce with a portion of roast beef, and some tomato slices. Sprinkle with salt and pepper to taste, and then arrange a portion of potato salad on top. Tuck in the sides, and roll the tortillas firmly but gently, beginning with the filled side. Cut in half on the diagonal, and serve immediately.

NOTE: If using pita bread, insert a lettuce leaf and some tomato slices into the thin side of the pocket. Divide the roast beef into portions, and form each into a packet that will fit inside the pita. Tuck the packet inside the bread, and top the roast beef with the potato salad.

Antipasto Wrap

It will take longer for the deli department to slice the salami and cheese than it will to assemble these wraps. *Serves 6*

SUGGESTED WRAPPERS: Pita bread ◎ eight-inch flour tortillas

One 4-ounce jar marinated artichoke
    hearts, sliced, with marinade
    reserved
2 jarred roasted red bell peppers,
    drained and cut into 1-inch strips
6 large romaine or Boston lettuce leaves
6 slices Italian Fontina
¼ pound thinly sliced mortadella

¼ pound thinly sliced salami
¼ pound thinly sliced coppa or
    soppressata
3 plum tomatoes, cored, seeded, and
    thinly sliced
6 slices fresh mozzarella
Freshly ground black pepper

1. Combine the sliced artichoke hearts and their marinade with the bell pepper slices, and set aside.

2. Line one side of each pita pocket with a lettuce leaf, and then layer the Fontina, mortadella, and salami on top of the lettuce. Insert a portion of artichoke and pepper mixture, with some of its dressing, and then layer the coppa, tomatoes, and mozzarella. No salt will be needed, since the meats contain salt, but sprinkle the cheese with pepper to taste. Serve immediately.

NOTE: If using flour tortillas, place a lettuce leaf on one edge, leaving a 1½-inch margin on both sides. Layer the wrap ingredients as detailed above. Tuck the sides around the filling, then roll the tortillas firmly but gently, beginning with the filled side. Cut in half on the diagonal, and serve immediately.

Pico de Gallo Wrap

In Spanish, *pico de gallo* means "rooster's beak," which bears no relationship to this refreshing salad that contrasts sweet oranges and crunchy jicama with a spicy chile dressing. *Serves 6*

SUGGESTED WRAPPERS: Eight-inch flour tortillas ◎ pita bread

¼ cup freshly squeezed lime juice
1 teaspoon chile powder
1 to 2 teaspoons finely chopped
    jalapeño or serrano chile
1 garlic clove, peeled and crushed
1 teaspoon sugar
Salt and freshly ground black pepper

⅓ cup vegetable oil
1 jicama, about ¾ pound
3 seedless oranges
1 large cucumber, peeled, halved,
    seeded, and cut into ¼-inch slices
1 red bell pepper, seeds and ribs
    removed, thinly sliced

1. Combine the lime juice, chile powder, jalapeño or serrano chile, garlic, sugar, salt and pepper to taste in a jar with a tight-fitting lid. Shake well. Add the oil, and shake again. Set aside.

2. Using a sharp paring knife, remove the outer brown peel from the jicama, and then remove the inner fibrous peel. Cut the jicama into ½-inch slices, and then cut each slice into ½-inch strips. Place the strips in a large mixing bowl.

3. Peel the oranges, and use a sharp serrated knife to slice off the white membrane surrounding the orange. Holding the orange over the mixing bowl to catch the juice, cut around the white membranes to release the orange sections. Place them in the bowl with the jicama, and add the cucumber and bell pepper slices. Toss the salad with the dressing.

4. Place a portion of salad on the bottom half of each tortilla, leaving a 1½-inch margin on one side. Tuck the sides over the filling, and roll the tortillas firmly but gently, beginning with the filled side. Serve immediately.

NOTE: If using pita bread, cut the jicama slices in half to shorten them. Then stuff the salad into the pocket. The salad can be made up to 1 day in advance and refrigerated, tightly covered.

Homemade Chile Powder

Chile powder is nothing more that a blend of spices. Making your own allows you to control the flavor and intensity. Here is my preferred recipe: Combine 2 tablespoons ground red chile pepper, 2 tablespoons paprika, 1 tablespoon ground coriander, 1 tablespoon garlic powder, 1 tablespoon onion powder, 2 teaspoons ground cumin, 2 teaspoons cayenne, 1 teaspoon ground black pepper, and 1 teaspoon dried oregano. Store in a tightly covered jar in a cabinet.

Thai Cucumber and Pork Wraps

One of the great treats of Thai cuisine is the sweet/sour/hot cucumber pickles served as condiments with many dishes. For this wrap, marinated cucumbers are joined with other crunchy vegetables and mild but flavorful roast pork, which absorbs the flavor nicely. *Serves 6*

SUGGESTED WRAPPERS: Eight-inch flour tortillas ☺ rice paper pancakes

¾ cup distilled white vinegar

¼ cup firmly packed light brown sugar

1 tablespoon Vietnamese fish sauce

1 to 2 teaspoons dried red pepper flakes

1 English cucumber, trimmed, and very thinly sliced; or 2 regular cucumbers, peeled, halved, seeded, and very thinly sliced

3 plum tomatoes, cored, seeded, and thinly sliced

2 dozen snow peas, stemmed and thinly sliced

1 pound roast pork, thinly sliced

1 cup fresh bean sprouts, rinsed

1 red bell pepper, seeds and ribs removed, thinly sliced

1. Combine the vinegar, brown sugar, fish sauce, and pepper flakes in a mixing bowl. Stir well to dissolve the sugar. Add the cucumbers, stir well, and set aside to marinate for 30 minutes. After 20 minutes, add the tomato slices to the marinade.

2. While the cucumbers are marinating, microwave the snow-pea slices for 45 seconds, or until they turn bright green. Immediately plunge them into ice water to stop the cooking action. Drain, and set aside.

3. Place the tortillas on a counter, and layer the pork over one half of each tortilla, leaving a 1½-inch margin on both sides. Remove the cucumbers and tomatoes from the marinade with a slotted spoon, drain well, and arrange a portion on top of the meat. Top with some snow peas, bean sprouts, and bell pepper strips. Tuck in the sides, and roll the tortillas firmly but gently, beginning with the filled side. Slice in half on the diagonal, and serve immediately.

NOTE: If using rice paper pancakes, follow the directions given for Spicy Pacific Rim Shrimp (page 11). The cucumbers can be prepared up to one day in advance and refrigerated, tightly covered. Do not add the tomato slices until just prior to serving.

Roast Pork with
Black Bean—Papaya Salsa

Salsa has now come full circle to its original meaning in Spanish—"sauce." This tomatoless version joins sweet succulent papaya with black beans and seasoning—a perfect combination with mildly seasoned roast pork. Or you could substitute leftover chicken or turkey in this wrap. *Serves 6*

SUGGESTED WRAPPERS: Eight-inch flour tortillas ◎ Boston or iceberg lettuce cups

1 ripe papaya, peeled, seeds discarded,
    and finely chopped
1/2 red bell pepper, seeds and ribs
    removed, finely chopped
2 scallions, white parts and 4 inches of
    green tops trimmed, thinly sliced
1 shallot, peeled and chopped
1 teaspoon minced garlic
Juice of 1 lime

2 tablespoons olive oil
1/8 teaspoon cayenne pepper
Pinch of salt
2 tablespoons chopped fresh cilantro
    leaves
One 15-ounce can black beans, drained
    and rinsed
1 pound roast pork, thinly sliced
Salt and freshly ground black pepper

    1. Place all the ingredients except the roast pork in a mixing bowl, and toss to combine. Allow to sit for 10 minutes to blend the flavors.

    2. Place the tortillas on a counter, and place a portion of pork along one edge of each, leaving a 1½-inch margin on both sides. Sprinkle the pork with salt and pepper to taste, and top the pork with a portion of salsa. Tuck in the sides to enclose the filling, and roll the tortillas firmly but gently, beginning with the filled side. Cut the rolls in half on the diagonal, and serve immediately.

NOTE: If using lettuce cups, slice the pork into 1-inch wide strips, and toss with the salsa. Divide the mixture among the lettuce cups, and roll. The salsa can be made a day in advance and refrigerated. Do not make it more than a day in advance or the onion flavor will become too strong.

Spinach Salad Wrap

Warm, wilted spinach salads are a perennial favorite, and make a perfect wrap filling. Add some chicken slices or boiled shrimp for a heartier wrap. *Serves 6*

SUGGESTED WRAPPERS: Ten-inch flour tortillas ◎ pita bread

1 pound fresh spinach, stemmed, rinsed, and dried
2 carrots, peeled and cut into thin strips
1 red bell pepper, seeds and ribs removed, cut into thin strips
1 red onion, peeled, halved, and cut into thin rings
1 pound bacon, fried crisp, drained and broken into 1-inch pieces, with grease reserved

Olive oil or vegetable oil, if needed
3 tablespoons honey
4 tablespoons Dijon mustard
¼ cup cider vinegar
Salt and freshly ground black pepper
3 large hard-cooked eggs, peeled and sliced

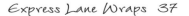

1. Combine the spinach, carrots, bell pepper strips, and onion in a mixing bowl. Pour the bacon grease into a measuring cup. Add oil, if necessary, to measure ½ cup.

2. Combine the honey, mustard, and vinegar in the pan used for frying the bacon. Season with salt and pepper to taste. Heat over medium high heat until the liquid comes to a boil, stirring with a spoon to dislodge the browned bits clinging to the bottom of the pan. Add the bacon grease, and return to a boil. Pour the dressing over the spinach salad, and toss.

3. Place the tortillas on a counter, and place a portion of salad on one edge of each, leaving a 2-inch margin on both sides. Top the salad with hard-cooked egg slices and reserved bacon pieces. Tuck in the edges to enclose the filling, and roll the tortillas tightly but gently, beginning with the filled edge. Cut the rolls in half on the diagonal, and serve immediately.

NOTE: If using pita bread, fill the pocket of each with the salad, and then insert slices of hard-cooked egg and bacon.

Egg Salad Pinwheels

Very finely chopped egg salad makes a perfect spread for pinwheels, since it can be flavored and layered in myriad ways. I often serve these sliced into sections with Bloody Marys or Champagne as brunch openers. *Makes 12 bread slices, or enough to serve 6 whole portions or up to 36 pieces*

6 large hard-cooked eggs, peeled and quartered

4 tablespoons mayonnaise

2 teaspoons sour cream

Salt and freshly ground black pepper

12 slices sandwich white bread, trimmed and rolled flat (page 9)

1. Place the eggs, mayonnaise, and sour cream in the bowl of a food processor fitted with the steel blade, and season with salt and pepper to taste. Using an on-and-off pulsing action, and scraping the sides of the bowl when necessary, chop the egg salad until it is almost a puree.

2. Spread 1 tablespoon egg mixture on each slice of flattened bread, and roll into pinwheels (page 9). Trim the ends, and cut into sections of desired length or keep whole. Serve immediately.

VARIATIONS: ◎ Add 1 teaspoon chopped fresh dill to the salad, and top with thinly sliced smoked salmon. Or add a few slices of salmon to the food processor bowl, and chop finely along with the eggs. ◎ Add 1 teaspoon curry powder to the salad, and top with thin slices of smoked turkey. ◎ Substitute tartar sauce for the mayonnaise, and top with morsels of crabmeat. ◎ Sprinkle the salad with red or black caviar after spreading it on the bread. ◎ Stir in 2 tablespoons finely chopped peeled and seeded tomato pulp. ◎ Substitute 1 tablespoon sun-dried tomato paste for 1 tablespoon mayonnaise. ◎ Add 6 pimiento-stuffed olives to the food processor bowl, and chop finely along with the eggs. ◎ Substitute Dijon mustard for the sour cream, and top with thinly sliced ham.

Grating Cheese Easily

To keep cheese from sticking to the grater, brush or spray a little oil on the grater, and the cheese will come off the grater easily.

Vegetable Antipasto Wrap

The antipasto table in an Italian restaurant dazzles the eyes before the palate even enters the picture. This wrap combines many of the wonderful colors, flavors, and textures of the vegetable offerings, and since the ingredients are so flavorful, only minimal dressing is necessary. *Serves 6*

SUGGESTED WRAPPERS: Pita bread ◎ eight-inch flour tortillas ◎ Armenian lavash

Two 4-ounce jars marinated artichoke hearts, drained with marinade reserved, and each one cut in half
3 jarred roasted red bell peppers, cut into 1-inch slices
1 cup olive salad, pitted and halved
1/2 cup chopped giardiniera vegetables
2 garlic cloves, peeled and minced
1/4 cup chopped fresh parsley

2 tablespoons olive oil
1/4 cup freshly grated Parmesan
6 slices provolone
2 cups firmly packed, stemmed, and rinsed fresh arugula leaves
3 plum tomatoes, cored, seeded, and thinly sliced
Salt and freshly ground black pepper

1. Combine the artichoke hearts, bell peppers, olive salad, giardiniera vegetables, garlic, parsley, and olive oil in a mixing bowl, along with the artichoke marinade. Toss gently to combine. Add the Parmesan, and toss again.

2. Place a slice of provolone on the thin side of each pita pocket, and top with arugula leaves and tomato slices. Spoon the vegetable mixture into the pita pocket, and serve immediately.

NOTE: If using tortillas or lavash, place the provolone slice on one edge, and top with arugula and tomato, leaving a 1 1/2-inch margin on one side. Place a portion of vegetable salad on top. Tuck over the sides to enclose the filling, and roll the wrappers firmly but gently, beginning with the filled side. Serve immediately.

Gazpacho Wrap

While gazpacho is really a soup, for years I have been making it more and more chunky and less pureed. So the next logical step is to not chop the soup ingredients at all, and serve the crunchy and garlicky-flavored vegetables as a wrap. *Serves 6*

SUGGESTED WRAPPERS: 10-inch flour tortillas ◎ pita bread

1 medium Bermuda or other sweet
    white onion, peeled, halved, and
    thinly sliced
2 cucumbers, peeled, seeded, and cut
    into long spears
1 green bell pepper, seeds and ribs
    removed, cut into long, thin slices
1 red bell pepper, seeds and ribs
    removed, cut into long, thin slices
6 medium to large tomatoes, peeled,
    seeded, and cut into thin wedges

5 garlic cloves, peeled and minced
2 teaspoons finely chopped jalapeño
    pepper or 1 teaspoon Tabasco
    sauce
1/4 cup sherry or red wine vinegar
Salt and freshly ground black pepper
1/2 cup extra virgin olive oil
1/4 cup chopped fresh cilantro leaves
    (optional)
Romaine or Boston lettuce leaves

1. Combine the onion, cucumbers, green and red bell peppers, and tomatoes in a large bowl. Combine the garlic, jalapeño, vinegar, and salt and pepper to taste in a jar with a tight-fitting lid, and shake well. Add the olive oil and cilantro, if used, and shake again. Pour the dressing over the vegetables, and toss well to coat.

2. Place the tortillas on a counter, and place a lettuce leaf and a portion of salad along one edge of each, leaving a 2-inch margin on both sides. Tuck in the sides to enclose the filling, and roll the tortillas firmly but gently, beginning at the filled edge. Cut in half on the diagonal, and serve immediately.

NOTE: If using pita bread, line the thin side of each pocket with a lettuce leaf, and then stuff in the salad. This salad improves in flavor if made a few hours in advance and refrigerated, tightly covered. Use within 6 hours, and do not make the wraps in advance.

A Chile Tip

To ensure that the potent chile oils do not come in contact with your hands while cutting or chopping, rub the hand not holding the knife with a thick coat of vegetable oil or vegetable shortening, or wear rubber gloves.

Meals in Minutes

Unlike the recipes in the preceding chapter, some ingredients for these dishes need cooking, but the total attended time—not counting how long it takes for foods to marinate or bake while you do something else—is under 20 minutes.

Many of these recipes wrap up everything you need for a total meal—including a portion of rice or pasta wrapped right along with the meats and vegetables. Garlicky Shrimp with Yellow Rice takes 5 minutes to prepare. Chicken Parmigiana is wrapped with angel hair pasta tossed with some traditional tomato sauce.

The rice or pasta can easily be omitted from a recipe if you prefer a lighter or less filling dish. For example, Stir-fried Chicken with Beans and Rice could easily omit the rice, as could Stir-fried Ginger Beef with String Beans.

Most of the recipes in this chapter are inspired by the popular and vibrantly flavorful cuisines of Asia, Latin America, and from the countries all along the sunny Mediterranean.

Of course, familiar, comfort foods can also be wrapped. You'll find that wrapping the components makes Barbecued Beef and Slaw Wrap a far less messy dish to eat.

Garlicky Shrimp with Yellow Rice

This easy shrimp wrap is based on a Spanish *tapa,* one of the "little dishes" served in bars throughout Spain, enjoyed with a predinner glass of sherry. The shrimp are ready in minutes, and the spicy, garlicky juices become a sauce for the rice. *Serves 6*

SUGGESTED WRAPPERS: Armenian lavash ◎ eight-inch flour tortillas

³/₄ cup olive oil

¹/₄ cup coarsely chopped garlic

1 tablespoon paprika

¹/₄ to ¹/₂ teaspoon dried red pepper flakes

1¹/₂ pounds medium shrimp, peeled and deveined

Salt and freshly ground black pepper

¹/₄ cup chopped fresh parsley

3 plum tomatoes, cored, seeded, and diced

3 tablespoons sliced pimiento-stuffed green olives

One 5-ounce package yellow rice, cooked according to directions, hot

1. Heat the olive oil in a large sauté pan or skillet over medium heat. Add the garlic, and sauté for 1 minute, stirring constantly, or until the garlic has begun to brown. Add the paprika and red pepper flakes, and sauté for 30 seconds. Raise the heat to medium high, and add the shrimp. Sauté for 2 to 3 minutes, or until the shrimp have turned pink. Season with salt and pepper to taste, and stir in the parsley.

2. Stir the tomatoes and olives into the rice.

3. Place the wrappers on a counter, and spoon a portion of rice on one edge of each, leaving a 1¹/₂-inch border on both sides. Tuck the sides over the filling, and roll wrappers firmly but gently, beginning with the filled edge. Cut in half on the diagonal, and serve immediately.

NOTE: The rice can be prepared up to a day in advance and refrigerated, tightly covered with plastic wrap. Reheat it in a microwave oven or over low heat.

Grilled Shrimp with Leeks, Bacon, and Wild Mushrooms

Grilled shrimp is enhanced by this creamy sauce of delicate leeks, woodsy wild mushrooms, and smoky bacon. This is an easy wrap, but certainly one worthy of a special occasion. *Serves 6*

SUGGESTED WRAPPERS: Eight-inch flour tortillas ☻ Armenian lavash

3 tablespoons unsalted butter, divided
6 leeks, white parts only, trimmed, cut into a fine julienne, and rinsed well
2 garlic cloves, peeled and minced
2 cups heavy cream
1/2 pound bacon, fried crisp and crumbled

Salt and freshly ground black pepper
1/4 pound fresh shiitake mushrooms, stemmed and thinly sliced
1 1/2 pounds medium shrimp, peeled and deveined
3 tablespoons olive oil

1. Light a charcoal or gas grill, or preheat the oven broiler.
2. Melt half the butter in a large skillet over low heat. Add the leeks and garlic, cover the pan, and cook for 10 minutes, stirring occasionally. Add the cream, raise the heat to medium high, and cook until reduced by 2/3, stirring often. Stir in the bacon, season with salt and pepper to taste, and set aside.
3. While the cream is reducing, heat the remaining butter in a medium skillet over medium high heat. Sauté the shiitakes until tender and brown. Stir the mushrooms into the sauce.
4. Brush the shrimp with oil, and season with salt and pepper to taste. Grill the shrimp for 1 to 2 minutes per side, or to desired doneness.
5. Place the wrappers on a counter. Place a portion of shrimp along one edge of

each, leaving a 1¹/₂-inch margin on both sides. Spoon the leek mixture over the shrimp. Tuck in the sides to enclose the filling, and roll wrappers firmly but gently, starting at the filled side. Cut in half, and serve immediately.

NOTE: Large sea scallops, cut into halves, can be used in place of the shrimp. The leek mixture can be prepared up to 2 days in advance and refrigerated, tightly covered. Reheat it in a microwave oven or over low heat in a small saucepan until hot. Stir in the bacon and grill the shrimp just prior to serving.

Indonesian Chicken with Pineapple Salsa

I once enjoyed a similar dish to this one while lounging on a beach in Bali, but here the curried barbecued chicken is wrapped in rice paper pancakes. *Serves 6*

SUGGESTED WRAPPERS: Rice paper pancakes ◎ eight-inch flour tortillas

¹/₂ ripe pineapple or one 20-ounce can crushed pineapple packed in juice and drained
¹/₄ cup firmly packed light brown sugar
1 to 2 teaspoons finely chopped serrano or jalapeño chile
2 tablespoons chopped fresh cilantro leaves
2 tablespoons freshly squeezed lime juice
¹/₃ cup ketchup

2 teaspoons curry powder
1¹/₂ pounds boneless skinless chicken breasts, pounded to an even ¹/₄-inch thickness, cut into ¹/₂-inch wide slices
12 leaves Boston or romaine lettuce leaves
3 scallions, white parts and 6 inches of green tops trimmed, and thinly sliced

1. Peel and core the pineapple, if using fresh fruit, and chop the flesh in a food processor fitted with the steel blade, using an on-and-off pulsing action. Combine the pineapple, brown sugar, chile, and ¼ cup water in a saucepan, and bring to a boil. Simmer over low heat uncovered, stirring occasionally, for 25 minutes, or until thickened. Remove the pan from the heat, and stir in the cilantro and lime juice.

2. Combine half the pineapple mixture with the ketchup and curry powder, and marinate the chicken slices for 30 minutes at room temperature, or up to 3 hours refrigerated.

3. Light a charcoal or gas grill, or preheat the oven broiler. Remove the chicken from the marinade, and grill or broil 3 to 4 minutes per side, or until the chicken is cooked through.

4. Fill a wide mixing bowl with very hot tap water. Place a damp tea towel in front of you on the counter. Place the rice paper pancakes on a plate, and cover with a barely damp towel. Line a baking sheet with plastic wrap.

5. Fill one rice paper pancake at a time, keeping the remainder covered. Totally immerse the pancake in the hot water for 2 seconds. Remove it and place it on the damp tea towel; it will become pliable within a few seconds. Gently fold the front edge of the pancake ⅓ of the way to the top. Place a section of lettuce leaf and some scallions on the folded portion, and top with some chicken slices and pineapple salsa, leaving a 1½-inch margin on each side. Fold the sides over the filling, and roll tightly but gently, beginning with the filled side. Take a second sheet of rice paper, and soften it. Place the filled roll in the center of the sheet, fold the sides over it, and roll it gently. Place the roll on the baking sheet, and continue to fill the rice paper pancakes in the same manner. Cut each roll in half on the diagonal, and serve immediately.

NOTE: If using flour tortillas, place a lettuce leaf along one edge, leaving a 1½-inch margin on both sides. Layer as above, then tuck in the sides to enclose the filling, and roll firmly but gently, beginning with the filled edge. The pineapple salsa can be prepared up to 3 days in advance and refrigerated, tightly covered with plastic wrap. Bring to room temperature or heat before wrapping.

Sarah's Spicy Carrots with Shredded Chicken

This recipe is adapted from my friend Sarah Leah Chase's *Nantucket Open House Cookbook*. While the dressing is highly spiced, the parsley makes it refreshing, and it brings out the sweetness of the carrots and adds zest to the chicken. *Serves 6*

SUGGESTED WRAPPERS: Pita bread ◎ eight-inch flour tortillas

1 pound carrots, peeled or scrubbed,
    trimmed, and cut on the diagonal
    into ¼-inch slices
¼ cup balsamic vinegar
¼ cup red wine vinegar
3 tablespoons sweet Hungarian paprika
2 tablespoons ground cumin

¼ teaspoon cayenne pepper
4 garlic cloves, peeled and crushed
⅔ cup finely chopped fresh parsley
Salt and freshly ground black pepper
½ cup olive oil
1 pound roasted chicken, thinly sliced

   1. Place the carrots in a large pot, and add cold water to cover. Bring the water to a boil, and cook over high heat until the carrots are crisp-tender, about 3 to 4 minutes. Drain immediately, and place the carrots in a mixing bowl.

   2. While the carrots are cooking, combine the balsamic vinegar, red wine vinegar, paprika, cumin, cayenne, garlic, and parsley along with salt and pepper to taste in a jar with a tight-fitting lid, and shake well. Add the oil to the jar, and shake again. Pour the dressing over the hot carrots, and toss to coat evenly.

   3. Line each pita bread with chicken slices, and then stuff the carrot salad into the pocket using a slotted spoon. Serve immediately.

NOTE: If using flour tortillas, place the chicken slices on one half of each tortilla, leaving a 1½-inch margin on both sides. Place a portion of carrots on top of the chicken.

Tuck in the sides to enclose the filling, and roll the tortillas firmly but gently, beginning with the filled side. Cut in half, and serve immediately. The salad can be made up to 1 day in advance and refrigerated, tightly covered. Allow it to reach room temperature before serving.

Stir-fried Crab and Spinach in Black Bean Sauce

Chinese fermented black beans give a distinctive, earthy and—I think—delicious flavor to seafood dishes, such as this easy crab and spinach stir-fry. With the addition of jasmine rice, this wrap becomes an entire meal. *Serves 6*

SUGGESTED WRAPPERS: Ten-inch flour tortillas ◎ Boston or iceberg lettuce cups

1 pound lump crabmeat
¼ cup vegetable oil
5 garlic cloves, peeled and minced
2 tablespoons finely chopped fresh
    ginger
½ cup chopped scallions, white parts
    and 4 inches of green tops, divided

3 tablespoons fermented black beans,
    rinsed and chopped
3 tablespoons oyster sauce
4 cups tightly packed, stemmed and
    rinsed fresh spinach
2 teaspoons cornstarch
2 cups cooked jasmine rice, hot

    1. Spread the crab out on a plate, and go over it carefully with your fingers to remove any bits of shell. Set aside.

    2. Heat the oil in a wok or large skillet over medium high heat. Add the garlic, ginger, and half the scallions. Stir-fry for 30 seconds. Add the black beans and oyster sauce, and stir well. Add the spinach, raise the heat to high, and stir-fry for 1 to 2 minutes, or until the spinach is wilted. Reduce the heat to low, and gently stir in the crab. Mix the cornstarch with 3 tablespoons cold water, and add it to the pan. Simmer for 1 minute, stirring gently, or until the mixture comes to a simmer and has lightly thickened.

3. Place the tortillas on a counter, and place a portion of rice along one edge of each, leaving a 2-inch margin on both sides. Divide the crab mixture over the rice, sprinkle with the remaining scallions, tuck the sides around the filling, and roll tortillas firmly but gently, beginning with the filled side. Cut in half on the diagonal, and serve immediately.

NOTE: If using lettuce cups, place a heaping tablespoon of rice in each, top with crab, and sprinkle with scallions. Tuck in the sides, and roll. Medium shrimp can be substituted for the crab. Add the shelled and deveined shrimp to the pan with the black beans, and stir-fry for 1 minute before continuing with the recipe.

Chicken Parmigiana

An Italian-American favorite all wrapped and rolled. No side of spaghetti is needed.
Serves 4 to 6

SUGGESTED WRAPPERS: Pita bread ◎ Armenian lavash

3/4 cup vegetable oil, divided
2 teaspoons minced garlic
Salt and freshly ground black pepper
1 teaspoon dried Italian seasoning
1/3 cup Italian-seasoned bread crumbs
1/4 cup grated Parmesan
1 1/2 pounds boneless, skinless chicken
    breasts, pounded to an even
    1/2-inch thickness, then cut into
    3-inch wide strips

3/4 cup spaghetti sauce, hot
1 cup grated mozzarella
12 thin slices prosciutto

1. Preheat the oven to 425°F. Pour ½ cup oil into a 9 × 13-inch baking pan, and place in the oven for 5 minutes to heat.

2. Pour the remaining oil into a mixing bowl. Add the garlic, salt and pepper to taste, and Italian seasoning. Mix the bread crumbs with the Parmesan on a sheet of plastic wrap or waxed paper. Dip the sliced chicken breasts in the oil mixture and then in the crumbs, patting the crumbs onto the chicken breasts.

3. Remove the hot pan from the oven, and add the chicken in a single layer. Bake for 10 minutes, turn gently with a slotted spatula, and bake 6 minutes more. Remove the chicken from the pan, and drain well on paper towels.

4. Reduce the oven to 400°F. Cover a baking sheet with heavy-duty aluminum foil. Tuck the chicken slices into the pita pockets, and spoon in some sauce and mozzarella. Insert 2 slices of prosciutto over the cheese in each pita.

5. Place the pitas on the baking sheet, and bake the wrapped chicken in the oven for 6 minutes, or until the cheese is melted. Serve immediately.

NOTE: If using lavash, place the wrappers on a counter, and place a portion of chicken on one edge of each wrapper, leaving a 1½-inch margin on both sides. Spoon some sauce over the chicken, and sprinkle mozzarella over the sauce, and top with 2 slices prosciutto. Tuck the sides of the lavash around the filling, and roll tightly. The chicken can be prepared up to 2 hours in advance and kept at room temperature. Do not assemble the wraps until just prior to serving.

To Flatten Chicken Cutlets

Space boneless chicken breasts 4 inches apart between sheets of plastic wrap. Pound them with the bottom of a heavy skillet to the desired thickness.

Stir-fried Chicken in Mustard Sauce with Dried Apricots

From Chinese pork to Austrian stuffed cabbage, sweet and sour is one of the world's most popular flavor combinations. Dried apricots give this chicken wrap a sweet flavor, while the mustard and vinegar provide the acid. *Serves 6*

SUGGESTED WRAPPERS: Ten-inch flour tortillas ◎ Armenian lavash

1½ pounds boneless, skinless chicken
    breasts, pounded to an even ½-
    inch thickness, and cut into strips
    1 inch wide and 3 inches long
Salt and freshly ground black pepper
All-purpose flour for dusting
¼ cup vegetable oil
1 medium onion, peeled and diced

2 teaspoons minced garlic
2 carrots, peeled and cut on the
    diagonal into ¼-inch slices
¼ cup finely chopped dried apricots
¾ cup chicken stock
1 tablespoon white wine vinegar
2 tablespoons grainy mustard
2 cups cooked jasmine rice, hot

    1. Season the chicken slices with salt and pepper to taste, and dust with flour, shaking off any excess over the sink.

    2. Heat the oil in a large skillet over medium high heat. Add the chicken slices to the pan, and brown them on both sides, turning gently; this may have to be done in a few batches. Remove the slices from the pan with a slotted spatula, and set aside.

    3. Reduce the heat to medium, add the onion and garlic to the pan, and sauté, stirring frequently, for 5 minutes. Return the chicken to the pan, and add the carrots, apricots, stock, vinegar, and mustard. Bring to a boil, and cook over medium heat for 5 to 7 minutes, stirring occasionally, or until the meat and vegetables are cooked through and the sauce has thickened. Season with salt and pepper to taste.

4. Place the wrappers on a counter. Spoon a portion of rice on one edge of each, leaving a 1¹/₂-inch margin on both sides. Divide the chicken mixture into 6 portions and place on top of the rice. Tuck in the sides to enclose the filling, and roll the wrappers firmly but gently, beginning with the filled side. Cut each in half on the diagonal, and serve immediately.

NOTE: This recipe can also be made with thinly sliced veal cutlets, cut into strips 1 inch wide by 3 inches long.

Stir-fried Chicken Chili with Beans and Rice

A robust combination of chicken with beans and rice, this easy wrap has a mellow smokiness from the bacon as well as some spiciness provided by the chiles and salsa. *Serves 6*

SUGGESTED WRAPPERS: Ten-inch flour tortillas ◎ pita bread

¹/₄ pound bacon, cut into ¹/₂-inch pieces
1 pound boneless, skinless chicken
    breasts, trimmed and cut into
    ³/₄-inch cubes
Salt and freshly ground black pepper
1 tablespoon minced garlic
1 to 2 tablespoons finely chopped
    jalapeño pepper
1 tablespoon chile powder

1 cup tomato salsa
One 1-pound can kidney or pinto
    beans, drained and rinsed
¹/₃ cup chopped fresh cilantro leaves,
    divided
³/₄ to 1 cup chicken stock or water
2 cups cooked long-grain rice, hot
¹/₂ cup crumbled *queso cotija* or freshly
    grated Parmesan (optional)

1. Place the bacon pieces in a large skillet over medium high heat. Cook until the bacon is crisp. Remove the bacon from the pan with a slotted spoon, and set aside.

2. Season the chicken pieces with salt and pepper to taste, and add them to the pan. Stir-fry the chicken over high heat, stirring constantly, for 3 minutes. Add the garlic and jalapeño to the pan, and stir-fry for 1 minute. Add the chile powder to the pan, and stir for 30 seconds.

3. Return the bacon to the pan, and add the salsa, kidney beans, half the cilantro, and the stock. Stir well, and bring to a boil. Reduce the heat to medium, and cook for 5 to 7 minutes, or until the liquid is reduced and the mixture has slightly thickened. Season with salt and pepper to taste.

4. To serve, place ⅓ cup rice in a line along one edge of each tortilla, leaving a 2-inch margin at both sides. Place a portion of chicken and beans on top of the rice, and sprinkle with the remaining cilantro and cheese, if desired. Tuck in the sides to enclose the filling, and roll each tortilla firmly but gently, beginning with the filled side. Cut in half on the diagonal and serve immediately.

NOTE: If using pita bread, cut off the tops and place the pitas on the counter. Spoon the rice into each pocket, and top with the chicken mixture. The chicken mixture and rice can be prepared up to 1 day in advance and refrigerated, tightly covered. Reheat them separately in a microwave oven or over low heat before wrapping.

Leftover Rice for Wraps

Store leftover rice in a heavy resealable plastic bag and refrigerate. To reheat, place the bag in a pan of boiling water for 3 to 5 minutes or microwave the rice in the bag on HIGH (100%) for 45 to 90 seconds, depending on the amount of rice.

Ranch Wrap

~~~

Spicy southwestern-style steak is the centerpiece of this wrap. Crunchy salad vegetables and Jalapeño Jack make it an all-in-one meal. *Serves 6*

SUGGESTED WRAPPERS: Eight-inch flour tortillas ◎ Armenian lavash

3 garlic cloves, peeled and minced
2 teaspoons chile powder
Salt and freshly ground black pepper
1½ pounds boneless sirloin steak, all visible fat trimmed
⅓ cup mayonnaise
¼ cup barbecue sauce

6 to 12 Boston or romaine lettuce leaves
3 plum tomatoes, cored, seeded, and thinly sliced
½ small red onion, peeled and thinly sliced
¼ pound Jalapeño Jack, grated

1. Light a charcoal or gas grill, or preheat the oven broiler. Combine the garlic and chile powder with salt and pepper to taste, and rub on both sides of the trimmed steak. Grill or broil the meat to desired doneness, and allow to rest for 10 minutes. Carve the meat into thin slices. While the meat is cooking, combine the mayonnaise and barbecue sauce.

2. Place the wrappers on a counter. Place some lettuce on one edge of each wrapper, leaving a 1½-inch margin on both sides. Spread a layer of barbecue mayonnaise over the lettuce, and then layer the tomato slices and onion. Top with a portion of steak, and sprinkle the hot meat with some grated cheese. Tuck in the sides to enclose the filling, and then roll firmly but gently, beginning with the filled side. Cut in half on the diagonal, and serve immediately.

NOTE: For a variation on this dish, use boneless, skinless chicken breast halves.

Sautéed Turkey with Prosciutto, Cheese, and Sage

Salty prosciutto, creamy cheese, and aromatic sage flavor many Italian dishes, including this wrap made with quick-cooking turkey breast cutlets. The addition of pasta makes for a complete handheld meal. *Serves 6*

SUGGESTED WRAPPERS: Ten-inch flour tortillas ◎ Armenian lavash

Vegetable oil spray
6 turkey breast cutlets (about 1½ pounds), cut into 3-inch strips
Salt and freshly ground black pepper
3 tablespoons olive oil
12 thin slices prosciutto
6 thin slices Fontina

18 fresh sage leaves or 2 teaspoons rubbed dried sage
1½ cups spaghetti sauce
One 9-ounce package fresh angel hair pasta, cooked according to directions

1. Preheat the oven to 400°F. Cover a baking sheet with heavy-duty aluminum foil. Spray the baking sheet with vegetable oil spray.

2. Season the turkey slices with salt and pepper to taste. Heat the oil in a large sauté pan or skillet over medium heat. Add the turkey, in batches if necessary, and cook for 3 minutes per side, turning once, or until golden on both sides.

3. Place the wrappers on a counter, and place a portion of sliced turkey on one edge of each wrapper, leaving a 2-inch margin on both sides. Top each portion of turkey with 2 slices prosciutto, 1 slice cheese, and 3 sage leaves. Mix the spaghetti sauce with the pasta, and place a portion of the mixture on top of the turkey. Tuck in the sides of the wrappers, and roll gently but firmly to enclose the filling.

4. Place the rolls on the baking sheet, seam side down, and spray the tops with vegetable oil spray. Bake in the preheated oven for 10 to 12 minutes, or until browned. Serve immediately.

NOTE: If making the dish without the pasta, reduce the amount of spaghetti sauce to ½ cup.

Grilled Flank Steak with Sautéed Onions and Shiitake Mushrooms

Sweet caramelized onions, woodsy mushrooms, and sharp blue cheese make this the perfect steak sandwich. Except for grilling the meat, everything can be prepared earlier in the day. *Serves 6*

SUGGESTED WRAPPERS: Pita bread ◎ ten-inch flour tortillas

1½ pounds flank steak
1 cup dry red wine
1 teaspoon dried Italian seasoning
1 tablespoon minced garlic
¾ cup olive oil, divided
1½ pounds onions, peeled and thinly sliced
½ pound fresh shiitake mushrooms, stemmed and sliced

Salt and freshly ground black pepper
¼ cup mayonnaise
¼ cup sour cream or plain yogurt
½ cup crumbled blue cheese
3 plum tomatoes, cored, seeded, and thinly sliced (optional)

1. Score the flank steak ¼ inch deep in a diamond pattern on both sides. Place the steak in a resealable plastic bag, then add the wine, Italian seasoning, garlic, and ¼ cup olive oil. Seal the bag, pushing out as much air as possible, and marinate the steak at room temperature for 2 hours, or refrigerated for up to 8 hours.

2. Light a charcoal or gas grill, or preheat the oven broiler. Place ¼ cup olive oil in a large sauté pan over medium high heat. Add the onions, and toss to coat. Cover the pan, and cook the onions over low heat for 10 minutes, stirring occasionally or until translucent. Uncover the pan, raise the heat to medium high, sprinkle the onions with salt, and cook the onions, stirring frequently, for 15 to 20 minutes, or until the onions are browned. Set aside.

3. Heat the remaining ¼ cup olive oil in a large sauté pan over medium high heat. Add the mushrooms, and sauté for 4 to 6 minutes, or until they are browned and soft. Sprinkle with salt and pepper to taste, and set aside. Combine the mayonnaise, sour cream, and blue cheese, and set aside.

4. Remove the meat from the marinade, and grill or broil it to desired doneness. Allow the meat to rest for 5 minutes before carving it into ¼-inch thick slices.

5. Spread the mayonnaise mixture on both sides of each pita pocket. Top with slices of steak, onions, and mushrooms along with tomato, if desired.

NOTE: If using tortillas, spread some of the blue cheese mixture on one side of each tortilla, leaving a 2-inch margin on both sides. Place a portion of meat along the edge, and top with onions, mushrooms, and tomato slices, if used. The onions, mushrooms, and sauce can be prepared up to a day in advance and refrigerated, tightly covered with plastic wrap. Reheat in a microwave oven or over low heat before serving. Broil steak just prior to serving.

Picadillo with Yellow Rice

Picadillo is similar to the chili served in the Southwest, or it can be used as a filling for empanadas. Its aromatic, sweet flavors come from the addition of raisins and cinnamon, which balance the fieriness of the chiles. *Serves 6*

SUGGESTED WRAPPERS: Eight-inch flour tortillas ◎ pita bread

1 pound lean ground beef
2 tablespoons vegetable oil
1 large onion, peeled and coarsely diced
2 garlic cloves, peeled and minced
1 tablespoon chile powder
1/4 teaspoon cinnamon
One 16-ounce can Mexican-style
    stewed tomatoes

1 tablespoon cider vinegar
1 4-ounce can chopped green chiles,
    drained
1/2 cup raisins
Salt and freshly ground black pepper
One 5-ounce package yellow rice,
    prepared according to package
    directions, hot

1. Place the beef in a large skillet over medium high heat. Brown the beef, breaking up any lumps, until it is evenly browned and no pink remains. Drain the beef in a sieve, and set aside. Wipe the pan out with paper towels, add the oil, and heat over medium heat. Add the onion and garlic, and sauté, stirring frequently, for 3 minutes, or until the onion is translucent. Add the chile powder and cinnamon to the pan, and cook for 30 seconds.

2. Return the beef to the pan. Add the tomatoes, vinegar, chiles, and raisins to the pan, and bring to a boil over medium heat. Reduce the heat slightly, and simmer the mixture for 20 minutes, or until thickened, stirring frequently. Season with salt and pepper to taste.

3. Place the tortillas on a counter, and spoon a portion of rice along one edge of each, leaving a 1 1/2-inch margin on both sides. Spoon a portion of picadillo on top of the rice. Tuck in the sides to enclose the filling, and roll the tortillas firmly but gently, beginning with the filled edge. Cut in half, and serve immediately.

If using pita bread, spoon a portion of rice onto the thin side of each pita pocket, and spoon the picadillo on top of it. The picadillo and rice can be prepared up to 2 days in advance and refrigerated, tightly covered. Reheat the components separately in a microwave oven or over low heat.

Stir-fried Ginger Beef with String Beans

Like all stir-fried dishes, this wrap is ready in minutes. The zing from the ginger and the crunch from the string beans are a great complement to the beef. To use leftover steak or roast beef, just marinate the meat for a few minutes, and then heat it through after the string beans are cooked. *Serves 6*

SUGGESTED WRAPPERS: Ten-inch flour tortillas ◎ pita bread

1½ pounds flank steak or well-trimmed
    sirloin steak, cut across the grain
    in ¼-inch slices
¼ cup oyster sauce
2 tablespoons sesame oil
1 tablespoon cornstarch
¼ cup vegetable oil
½ cup shredded fresh ginger
1 tablespoon minced garlic

¼ cup chopped scallions, white part
    and 4 inches of green tops
1 pound string beans, trimmed and cut
    on the diagonal into 1-inch pieces
2 tablespoons dry sherry
Salt and freshly ground black pepper
2 cups cooked jasmine rice, hot
    (optional)

1. Place the steak slices in a mixing bowl. Combine the oyster sauce, sesame oil, and cornstarch in a small bowl, and pour it over the meat. Allow the meat to marinate for 20 minutes.

2. Pour the vegetable oil into a wok or large skillet, and heat over high heat. Add the ginger, garlic, and scallions, and stir-fry for 30 seconds. Add the meat slices, and stir-fry for 2 minutes, separating the slices so that they all brown evenly. Add the string beans and sherry to the pan, and stir-fry for an additional 2 minutes, or until the beans are cooked but still crunchy and the meat is cooked to desired doneness. Add salt and pepper to taste.

3. If using rice, place a portion of rice along one edge of each tortilla, leaving a 2-inch margin on both sides, and top with a portion of beef. If not using rice, arrange the beef mixture on the tortilla in a similar manner. Tuck the sides of the tortillas around the filling, and roll them firmly but gently, beginning with the filled side. Cut in half on the diagonal, and serve immediately.

NOTE: If using pita bread, arrange a layer of rice, if desired, on one side of the bread, and place the meat mixture on top of the rice.

Barbecued Beef and Slaw Wrap

Here's my favorite way to use up leftover beef—from pot roast to roast beef and grilled hamburgers. The ginger, and lemon-scented sauce is easy to make from bottled barbecue sauce, and the cole slaw adds crunchy texture to this spicy beef wrap. *Serves 6*

SUGGESTED WRAPPERS: Pita bread ◎ eight-inch flour tortillas

1½ **cups barbecue sauce**	**Salt and freshly ground black pepper**
1 **lemon, thinly sliced**	1 **pound cole slaw**
2 **tablespoons chopped fresh ginger**	¼ **cup chopped red onion**
1 **tablespoon minced garlic**	¼ **cup chopped red bell pepper**
2½ **cups chopped cooked beef**	½ **teaspoon celery seed**

1. Combine the barbecue sauce, lemon, ginger, and garlic in a saucepan, and bring to a boil over medium heat. Reduce the heat to low, and simmer the sauce for 15 minutes. Strain the sauce, and return it to the saucepan. Add the beef, and bring to a boil over medium heat. Reduce the heat, and simmer the beef in the sauce for 10 minutes, stirring occasionally. Season with salt and pepper to taste, and keep warm.

2. Combine the slaw with the onion, red bell pepper, and celery seed.

3. Spoon a portion of meat into the thicker side of the pita pocket, and then top with a portion of slaw. Serve immediately.

NOTE: If using tortillas, place a portion of beef along one edge of each tortilla, leaving a 1½-inch margin on both sides. Top the beef with the slaw. Tuck the sides of the tortilla around the filling, and then roll the tortilla firmly but gently, beginning on the filled side. Cut in half, and serve immediately. The beef mixture can be prepared up to 2 days in advance and refrigerated, tightly covered. Reheat over low heat or in a microwave oven before wrapping.

Med-Rim Meatball Wrap
with Couscous

The distinctive flavors of North African food are gaining popularity as interest in Mediterranean cuisine moves beyond Italy, Greece, and southern France. Aromatic cinnamon and earthy cumin are the dominant notes in this meatball hero wrap, and the sauce moistens the couscous. *Serves 6*

SUGGESTED WRAPPERS: Pita bread ◎ Armenian lavash

1½ pounds ground beef
2 large onions, peeled and chopped, divided
⅔ cup chopped fresh parsley, divided
1 tablespoon chile powder
½ teaspoon cinnamon

Salt and cayenne pepper
¼ cup olive oil
4 garlic cloves, peeled and minced
Two 8-ounce cans tomato sauce
2 teaspoons ground cumin
2 cups cooked couscous, hot

1. Preheat the oven to 500°F. Line a 9 × 13-inch baking pan with heavy-duty aluminum foil.

2. Place the beef in a large mixing bowl, and add half the onions, half the parsley, chile powder, cinnamon, and salt and cayenne to taste. Mix well. Form the mixture into meatballs about the size of walnuts, and place them in the baking pan. Bake in the preheated oven for 10 minutes to brown.

3. While the meatballs are baking, heat the olive oil in a large skillet over medium heat. Add the remaining onions along with the garlic, and sauté, stirring frequently, for 3 minutes. Add the tomato sauce, remaining parsley, and cumin, and bring to a boil. Season with salt and cayenne to taste.

4. Remove the meatballs from the baking pan with a slotted spoon, and add them to the sauce. Bring to a boil, and simmer the meatballs, uncovered, turning occasionally with a slotted spoon, for 15 minutes.

5. Place a portion of couscous in the pocket of each pita bread, and spoon the meatballs and sauce on top. Serve immediately.

NOTE: If using in lavash, place a portion of couscous along one edge, leaving a 2-inch margin on both sides. Place the meatballs on top of the couscous, tuck in the sides, and roll the lavash firmly but gently from the filled side. Slice in half, and serve. The meatballs and sauce can be prepared up to 2 days in advance and refrigerated, tightly covered. Reheat over a low flame or in a microwave oven before wrapping.

Meatball Wrap with Apples and Cabbage

I think of this wrap as an "Eastern European hero," since its sweet and sour flavor is similar to that of traditional stuffed cabbage. Apples and raisins add fruity accents to this hearty dish. It's a great meal for a chilly fall day. *Serves 6*

SUGGESTED WRAPPERS: Pita bread ◎ Armenian lavash

1 pound ground beef
1 small onion, peeled and grated
2 garlic cloves, peeled and crushed
1 cup cooked rice (instant can be used)
Salt and freshly ground black pepper
½ pound shredded green cabbage

Two 8-ounce cans tomato sauce
⅓ cup firmly packed dark brown sugar
½ cup cider vinegar
½ cup raisins
1 Granny Smith apple, peeled, cored, and thinly sliced

1. Preheat the oven to 500°F. Line a 9 × 13-inch baking pan with heavy-duty aluminum foil. Bring a large saucepan of salted water to a boil.

2. Combine the beef, onion, garlic, and rice in a large mixing bowl. Season with salt and pepper to taste. Form the mixture into balls the size of walnuts, and place them in the baking pan. Bake the meatballs in the preheated oven for 10 minutes to brown.

3. While the meatballs are baking, blanch the cabbage in the boiling water for 5 minutes. Drain well, pressing with the back of a spoon to extract as much water as possible, and set aside.

4. Combine the tomato sauce, brown sugar, and vinegar in a large skillet. Stir well, and bring to a boil over medium heat. Add the raisins, apple slices, and cabbage to the pan along with the browned meatballs. Bring to a boil, and simmer over medium heat, uncovered, for 15 minutes, turning the meatballs gently with a slotted spoon a few times, or until the meatballs are cooked through and the sauce has reduced slightly.

5. Spoon equal portions of meatballs, apples, and cabbage into the pita pockets with a slotted spoon. Serve immediately.

NOTE: If using lavash, place the meatballs along one edge of each wrapper, leaving a 1½-inch margin on the sides. Tuck in the sides, and roll the lavash firmly but gently around the filling. Slice in half, and serve immediately. The meatball mixture can be made up to 2 days in advance and refrigerated, tightly covered. Reheat it over low heat or in a microwave oven before wrapping.

Pork Satay with Peanut Sauce

While Americans connect peanut butter with jelly, Asians use it as the basis for a spicy sauce that goes perfectly with marinated and grilled foods. The peanut butter sauce in this wrap is thick, and its intense flavor is fabulous with the pork. *Serves 6*

SUGGESTED WRAPPERS: Rice paper pancakes ◎ eight-inch flour tortillas

1 pound teriyaki-marinated pork tenderloin, at room temperature, trimmed; or marinate the tenderloin in a commercial teriyaki sauce marinade for 3 hours at room temperature (see Note)

½ cup chunky peanut butter

2 tablespoons coconut milk or light cream

2 tablespoons soy sauce

1 tablespoon rice wine vinegar

2 teaspoons chile paste with garlic or ½ to 1 teaspoon Tabasco sauce and ½ teaspoon minced garlic

2 tablespoons firmly packed dark brown sugar

2 teaspoons grated fresh ginger

2 tablespoons sesame oil

½ cup thinly sliced scallions, white parts and all of green tops

1 cup thinly sliced bok choy

1. Preheat the oven to 450°F. Line a 9 × 13-inch baking pan with heavy-duty aluminum foil. Place the pork tenderloin in the pan, and tuck the thin tail under so that the meat has an even shape all around. Bake for 15 minutes at 450°F., then reduce the temperature to 350°F. and roast for an additional 15 minutes, or until an instant-read meat thermometer inserted in the meat registers 145°F. Remove the meat from the oven, and allow it to rest for 10 minutes. Carve the meat into ¼-inch slices, and pour any juices that accumulate over the meat.

2. While the meat is roasting, prepare the peanut sauce. Combine the peanut butter, coconut milk, soy sauce, vinegar, chile paste, brown sugar, ginger, and sesame oil in a microwave-safe bowl or small saucepan. Microwave on HIGH (100%) power for 30 seconds. Stir until smooth, microwaving a bit longer if needed to heat the mixture. If using a saucepan, heat over low heat, stirring frequently. Set aside.

3. Fill a wide mixing bowl with very hot tap water. Place a damp tea towel in front of you on the counter. Place the rice paper pancakes on a plate, and cover with a barely damp towel. Line a baking sheet with plastic wrap.

4. Fill one rice paper pancake at a time, keeping the remainder covered. Totally immerse the pancake in the hot water for 2 seconds. Remove it and place it on the damp tea towel; it will become pliable within a few seconds. Gently fold the front edge of the pancake ⅓ of the way to the top. Place a few pork slices on the folded portion, leaving a 1½-inch margin on each side. Spread the pork with peanut sauce, and then sprinkle it with scallions and top with a few bok choy slices. Fold the sides of the pancake over the filling, and roll tightly but gently, beginning with the filled side. Take a second sheet of rice paper, and soften it. Place the filled roll in the center of the sheet, fold the sides of the second sheet over it, and roll gently. Place the roll on the baking sheet, and continue to fill the rice paper pancakes in the same manner. Cut each roll in half on the diagonal, and serve immediately.

NOTE: If using tortillas, spread peanut sauce on half of each tortilla, leaving a 1½-inch margin on both sides. Place a portion of pork on one edge of the tortilla, and top with scallions and bok choy. Tuck in the sides to enclose the filling, and roll the tortillas firmly but gently, beginning with the filled side. Cut in half on the diagonal, and serve immediately. The pork can be roasted and the sauce can be prepared up to 2 days in advance and refrigerated, tightly covered. Reheat the pork and sauce in a microwave oven until warm.

Roast Pork with Mashed Sweet Potatoes and Cinnamon Apples

This wrap reminds me of a bountiful Southern table. Mild roast pork, maple-scented sweet potatoes, and fried apples are a great combination, and so easy to prepare. *Serves 6*

SUGGESTED WRAPPERS: Ten-inch flour tortillas ◎ Armenian lavash

Vegetable oil spray
1½ pounds roast pork, thinly sliced
Two 1-pound cans sweet potatoes, drained
1 stick (¼) unsalted butter, divided
¼ cup maple syrup

Salt and freshly ground black pepper
3 cooking apples, such as Granny Smith, cored and cut into thin slices
⅓ cup sugar
1 teaspoon cinnamon

1. Preheat the oven to 400°F. Cover a large baking sheet with heavy-duty aluminum foil. Spray the foil with vegetable oil spray. Trim the pork of fat, and set aside.

2. Place the sweet potatoes in the bowl of a food processor fitted with the steel blade, and puree. Melt half the butter in a medium saucepan over low heat. Add the sweet potato puree, maple syrup, and salt and pepper to taste. Cook over low heat, stirring frequently, until the potatoes are hot. Set aside.

3. Place the remaining butter in a large skillet, and melt over medium heat. Add the apple slices, and sprinkle with sugar and cinnamon. Cook the apples over medium heat, stirring frequently, for 10 minutes, or until they are soft and slightly brown. If the sugar begins to turn brown, lower the heat.

4. To serve, spread a thick layer of sweet potato mixture on the bottom third of each wrapper, leaving a 2-inch margin on the sides. Top it with a layer of sliced pork and then one of apples. Tuck the sides of the wrapper around the filling and, beginning with the filled edge, roll the wrapper gently but firmly.

5. Arrange the rolls on the baking sheet seam side down, and spray the tops with vegetable oil. Place the rolls in the preheated oven for 10 minutes, or until lightly browned. Cut in half on the diagonal, and serve immediately.

NOTE: The dish can be assembled up to a day in advance and refrigerated, tightly covered with plastic wrap. To serve, preheat the oven to 375°F., then bake for 15 to 20 minutes.

Bombay Burgers

Northern Indian food is known for its Persian touches of incorporating dried fruits and aromatic spices. This wrap, inspired by that tradition, adds fragrant basmati rice into the equation. *Serves 6*

SUGGESTED WRAPPERS: Pita bread ◎ eight-inch flour tortillas

1½ pounds ground lamb
½ cup finely chopped dried apricots
1 medium onion, peeled and finely
    chopped
2 teaspoons crushed garlic
1 egg, lightly beaten
2 tablespoons milk

⅓ cup plain bread crumbs
¼ cup chopped fresh parsley
1 tablespoon curry powder
Salt and freshly ground black pepper
½ cup basmati rice
1 cinnamon stick
¾ cup yogurt cheese (page 5)

    1. Preheat the oven to 400°F. Line a 9 × 13-inch baking pan with heavy-duty aluminum foil.

    2. Combine the lamb, apricots, onion, garlic, egg, milk, bread crumbs, parsley, and curry powder in a mixing bowl. Season with salt and pepper to taste. Form the mixture to conform to the shape of the wrapper. If using pita bread, form the mixture into rounds that are 1 inch smaller than the diameter of the bread; if using tortillas, form the mixture into 5-inch logs. Bake the lamb in the preheated oven for 20 minutes, or until brown and an instant-read meat thermometer inserted in the lamb reads 150°F.

3. Bring 1 cup salted water to a boil. Place the rice in a sieve, and rinse well. Add the rice to the boiling water along with the cinnamon stick. Stir, then cover the pan, reduce the heat to low, and boil the rice for 20 minutes, or until tender and the water is absorbed. Keep warm, and discard the cinnamon stick.

4. Place a portion of lamb in each pita pocket. Spread a heaping tablespoon of yogurt cheese on top of the lamb, and surround it with a portion of rice.

NOTE: If using tortillas, place a portion of lamb along one edge of each tortilla, leaving a 1$^{1}/_{2}$-inch margin on both sides. Top the lamb with the yogurt cheese and rice. Tuck in the sides to enclose the filling, and roll the tortillas firmly but gently, beginning with the filled side. Cut in half on the diagonal, and serve immediately. The lamb can be baked and the rice can be cooked up to 1 day in advance and refrigerated, tightly covered with plastic wrap. Reheat in a 300°F. oven, wrapped in heavy-duty aluminum foil, for 15 minutes, or until hot.

Softening Butter

To quickly soften frozen or cold butter, grate it through the large holes of a box grater. The butter will be at room temperature in just a few minutes.

Southwest Corn and Sausage Toss

There's an old country-and-western song that says, "There are just two things that money can't buy, and that's true love and homegrown tomatoes." I'd add fresh corn to the list, and this easy filling for a southwestern-style wrap uses both of these summer glories. *Serves 6*

SUGGESTED WRAPPERS: Eight-inch flour tortillas ◎ pita bread

4 ears fresh corn, shucked
2 tablespoons vegetable oil
1 pound bulk pork sausage
1 cup finely chopped red or green bell
  pepper
5 scallions, trimmed and finely chopped,
  white parts and 6 inches of the
  green tops

¼ cup freshly squeezed lime juice
¼ cup maple syrup
¼ cup finely chopped fresh cilantro
  leaves or parsley
Salt and freshly ground black pepper
6 to 12 romaine or Boston lettuce leaves
2 beefsteak tomatoes, cored, seeded,
  and diced

1. Light a charcoal or gas grill, or preheat the oven broiler. Bring a large pot of salted water to a boil.

2. Add the corn to the water, and when the water returns to a boil, turn off the heat. Let the corn sit, covered, for 5 minutes. Remove the corn from the pan, and rub it with the oil. Grill or broil for about 5 minutes, or until the ears are lightly brown. When cool enough to handle, cut all the kernels off the cobs with a sharp serrated knife, and set aside.

3. Cook the sausage in a large skillet over medium high heat, breaking up lumps with a fork. Cook until brown, and then combine the sausage and a few tablespoons of rendered fat with the corn, bell pepper, and scallions. Combine the lime juice with the maple syrup, and toss with the corn mixture. Add the cilantro, and season with salt and pepper to taste.

4. Place the tortillas on a counter, and place some lettuce along one edge of each, leaving a 1¹/₂-inch margin on both sides. Top the lettuce with some diced tomato, and sprinkle with salt and pepper. Mound a portion of the corn mixture on top of the tomato. Tuck in the sides to enclose the filling, and roll the tortillas firmly but gently, beginning with the filled edge. Cut in half, and serve immediately.

NOTE: If using pita bread, line the thin side of each pocket with lettuce leaves, and add a layer of diced tomato. Stuff in the corn mixture, and serve immediately. The filling can be made up to 2 days in advance and refrigerated, tightly covered. Do not add the cilantro until just before serving, and allow the corn to reach room temperature for a few hours to take the chill off, or reheat it to room temperature in a microwave oven.

Italian Sausage Wrap with Broccoli Rabe

Broccoli rabe—sometimes called by its Italian name, *rapini*—has a more pungent and zesty flavor than common broccoli. In this wrap it goes wonderfully with Italian sausage, and takes just minutes to prepare. *Serves 6*

SUGGESTED WRAPPERS: Pita bread ◎ Armenian lavash

1¹/₂ **pounds mild or hot Italian sausage links**
1 **pound broccoli rabe, washed well with stems trimmed**
2 **teaspoons minced garlic**

2 **tablespoons olive oil**
Salt and freshly ground black pepper
6 **slices Italian Fontina**
3 **plum tomatoes, cored, seeded, and thinly sliced**

1. Prick the sausages with the tip of a paring knife. Place them in a large skillet and add ⅛ inch water. Place the skillet, covered, over high heat, and cook the sausages for 5 minutes. Reduce the heat to medium, uncover the pan, and cook the sausages, turning often, for another 5 to 7 minutes, or until they are brown and no pink remains. Remove them from the pan, cut them into thin slices, and keep warm. Pour the grease out of the pan, but do not wash the pan.

2. While the sausages are cooking, prepare the broccoli rabe. Tear the leaves off the stalks, and cut the stalks into 2-inch pieces.

3. Add the garlic and olive oil to the skillet in which the sausages were cooked. Sauté for 1 minute over medium heat, stirring constantly. Add the rabe stalks to the pan with 2 tablespoons water. Cover the pan and cook for 3 minutes. Stir well, add the leaves to the pan, and cook for another 3 minutes, adding more water if necessary so that the greens are not totally dry. Add salt and pepper to taste.

4. Insert 1 slice cheese into each pita pocket, and top with some tomato slices. Stuff in a portion of greens and sausage, and serve immediately.

NOTE: If using lavash, place a portion of greens along one edge of each wrapper, leaving a 1½-inch margin on both sides. Top the greens with the sausage, and then the cheese and tomato. Tuck in the sides to enclose the filling, and roll the lavash firmly but gently, beginning with the filled edge. Cut in half, and serve immediately. The sausages and greens can be prepared up to a day in advance and refrigerated, tightly covered. Reheat over low heat until hot before wrapping.

Grilled Sausage with Tomato—Mustard Vegetables and Cheese

This is the best "sausage hero" wrap you'll ever eat, with some sharp mustard spiking the tomato-flavored vegetable mix. While I like kielbasa, try making it with your favorite sausage. *Serves 6*

SUGGESTED WRAPPERS: Pita bread ◎ eight-inch flour tortillas

1½ pounds kielbasa or other smoked
    sausage
⅓ cup olive oil, divided
2 cups sliced mushrooms
Salt and freshly ground black pepper
2 onions, peeled and thinly sliced
2 tablespoons minced garlic

1 large green bell pepper, seeds and ribs
    removed, thinly sliced
¼ cup Dijon mustard
One 8-ounce can tomato sauce
¼ cup chopped fresh parsley
6 slices Swiss or Gruyère

   1. Light a charcoal or gas grill, or preheat the oven broiler. Heat half the olive oil in a large skillet over medium high heat. Add the mushrooms, and sauté, stirring constantly, for 5 minutes, or until they are cooked and browned. Season with salt and pepper to taste, remove mushrooms from the pan, and set aside. Pour the remaining oil into the skillet, and heat it over medium heat. Add the onions and garlic, and toss to coat. Cover the pan, reduce the heat to low, and cook for 5 minutes.

   2. Uncover the pan, raise the heat to medium high, and add the green pepper to the pan. Sauté, stirring frequently, for 5 to 7 minutes, or until the pepper slices are cooked. Stir in the mustard and tomato sauce, and add the mushrooms to the pan. Bring to a boil, and simmer over low heat, uncovered, for 5 minutes. Season with salt and pepper to taste, and stir in the parsley. Set aside and keep warm.

3. Prick the sausages with the points of a meat fork or the tip of a sharp paring knife. Grill or broil them until they are brown on all sides and no pink remains in the center. Cut the sausages on the diagonal into $1/4$-inch slices.

4. Place 1 slice cheese into the pocket of each pita. Tuck in sausage slices, and then spoon in some of the vegetable mixture. Serve immediately.

NOTE: If using flour tortillas, shred the cheese. Place a portion of sausage and vegetables on one edge of each tortilla, leaving a $1^{1/2}$-inch margin on both sides. Sprinkle with the shredded cheese, tuck in the sides to enclose the filling, and roll the tortillas firmly but gently, beginning with the filled edge. Cut in half and serve immediately. The sausages and the onion mixture can be prepared 1 day in advance and refrigerated, tightly covered. Reheat them in a microwave oven or in a skillet over low heat before wrapping.

Italian Eggplant Wraps

This Mediterranean-style wrap uses eggplant slices, topped with Italian cheese and meat and moistened with tomato sauce. It makes a great comfort food for wintry days. *Serves 6*

SUGGESTED WRAPPERS: Armenian lavash ◎ pita bread

1 small eggplant, cut into $1/2$-inch slices
Vegetable oil spray
All-purpose flour for dredging
2 large eggs
2 tablespoons milk
Salt and freshly ground black pepper

$1/2$ cup plain or Italian-flavored bread crumbs
$1/2$ cup vegetable oil
6 slices mozzarella or provolone
$1/4$ pound thinly sliced prosciutto
$1/4$ pound thinly sliced baked ham
$1/3$ cup tomato sauce or spaghetti sauce

1. Sprinkle the eggplant slices on both sides with salt. Place the eggplant slices on a triple layer of paper towels on the counter, cover with additional paper towels, and place a baking sheet over the slices. Weight the baking sheet with cans or bottles. Allow the eggplant to sit for 15 minutes.

2. Preheat the oven to 375°F. Cover a baking sheet with heavy-duty aluminum foil, and spray it with vegetable oil spray. Dip the eggplant slices in flour, shaking them over the sink to remove any excess. Beat the eggs with the milk, add salt and pepper to taste, and dip the eggplant slices in this mixture and then in the bread crumbs.

3. Heat the oil in a large skillet to a temperature of 375°F. Fry the eggplant slices for 2 to 3 minutes, or until golden brown. Turn gently with tongs, and fry the second side. Remove, and drain on paper towels, patting the tops. Repeat until all the eggplant is fried, adding more oil if necessary.

4. Place the lavash on a counter, and arrange eggplant slices on one edge, leaving a 1½-inch margin on both sides. Top the eggplant with a slice each of cheese, prosciutto, and ham, and 1 tablespoon tomato sauce. Tuck in the sides to enclose the filling, and roll the lavash firmly but gently, beginning with the filled edge. Place the rolls on the baking sheet, seam side down, and spray the top with oil.

5. Bake for 7 to 10 minutes, or until the cheese is melted. Cut in half on the diagonal, and serve immediately.

NOTE: If using pita bread, arrange the eggplant on the thicker side of the pocket, and layer as detailed above.

Cajun Wrap

Spicy sausage and beans are at the heart of Cajun cooking, and it takes just minutes to prepare this wrap. All you need is zydeco music and some cold beer to transport you to the bayous of Louisiana. *Serves 6*

SUGGESTED WRAPPERS: Eight-inch flour tortillas ◎ pita bread

2 tablespoons olive or vegetable oil
1 pound andouille sausage, sliced
    ¼ inch thick
1 cup diced onion
1 tablespoon minced garlic
1 red bell pepper, seeds and ribs
    removed, chopped

One 8-ounce can tomato sauce
1 to 2 teaspoons Tabasco sauce
One 1-pound can kidney beans, drained
    and rinsed
Salt and freshly ground black pepper
1½ to 2 cups cooked long-grain rice,
    hot

1. Heat the olive oil in a large skillet over medium high heat. Add the sausage to the pan, and cook until the sausage is browned, stirring occasionally. Reduce the heat to medium, and add the onion, garlic, and bell pepper to the pan. Sauté for 3 minutes, stirring frequently, or until the onion is translucent.

2. Add the tomato sauce and Tabasco to the pan along with the kidney beans. Stir well, and bring to a boil over medium heat. Reduce the heat to low, and simmer the mixture for 15 minutes, or until slightly reduced and the vegetables are soft. Add salt and pepper to taste.

3. Place the tortillas on a counter, and spoon a portion of cooked rice along one edge, leaving a 1½-inch margin on both sides. Place a portion of the sausage and bean mixture on top of the rice. Tuck in the sides to enclose the filling, and roll the tortillas firmly but gently, beginning with the filled edge. Cut in half, and serve immediately.

NOTE: If using pita bread, place a portion of rice in the bottom of each pocket, and spoon in the sausage and bean mixture. Serve immediately. The sausage mixture and the rice can be cooked up to a day in advance and refrigerated, tightly covered with plastic wrap. Reheat in a microwave oven or over low heat before wrapping.

Southwestern Vegetable Stew with Mexican Rice

This hearty dish, with its colorful, flavorful mix of quickly cooked vegetables and Mexican rice, makes a wonderful vegetarian wrap. To make it nonvegetarian, add some diced cooked chicken or turkey to the pan at the end of the cooking time. *Serves 6*

SUGGESTED WRAPPERS: Eight-inch flour tortillas ◎ pita bread

¼ cup olive oil
1 large onion, peeled and diced
3 garlic cloves, peeled and minced
1 medium zucchini, cut into ½-inch dice
1 red bell pepper, seeds and ribs removed, cut into thin strips
1 tablespoon chile powder

1 cup fresh or frozen corn kernels
One 1-pound can red kidney beans, drained and rinsed
¾ cup tomato salsa
Salt and freshly ground black pepper
One 5-ounce package Mexican rice, cooked according to directions, hot

1. Heat the olive oil in a large skillet over medium heat. Add the onion and garlic, and sauté, stirring frequently, for 3 minutes. Add the zucchini and bell pepper, raise the heat to medium high, and sauté for 2 minutes. Stir in the chile powder, and cook for 1 minute.

2. Add the corn, kidney beans, and salsa to the pan, and bring to a boil. Reduce the heat to medium, and simmer for 5 minutes, stirring occasionally, or until the corn is cooked and the liquid is slightly reduced. Season with salt and pepper to taste.

3. Place a portion of rice along one edge of each tortilla, leaving a 1½-inch margin on both sides. Spoon a portion of vegetable stew on top of the rice. Tuck the sides of the tortillas around the filling, and roll the tortillas firmly but gently, beginning with the filled edge. Cut each in half on the diagonal, and serve immediately.

NOTE: For pita bread, divide each portion of rice and vegetables in half, and spoon some rice into the pocket first. Then layer with stew, then rice, and top with a layer of stew. Stew and rice can be prepared up to 2 days in advance and refrigerated, tightly covered. Reheat in a microwave oven or over low heat before wrapping.

Creole Ham Wrap

This is a great way to use up leftover grilled or baked ham, sautéed with onion, green pepper, and tomato, in this Creole-inspired wrap. The trimmed glaze or sweet coating from the meat becomes the cook's treat to nibble! *Serves 6*

SUGGESTED WRAPPERS: Ten-inch flour tortillas ◎ pita bread

2 pounds cooked ham steak, about ½ inch thick
2 tablespoons olive oil
1 large onion, peeled and thinly sliced
3 garlic cloves, peeled and minced
One 1-pound can plum tomatoes packed in tomato puree, coarsely chopped

1 green bell pepper, seeds and ribs removed, thinly sliced
½ cup dry white wine
1 teaspoon dried thyme
3 tablespoons chopped fresh parsley
Salt
Cayenne pepper
2 cups cooked long-grain rice, hot

1. Trim the excess fat from the ham, and cut meat into 2-inch strips. Heat the olive oil in a large skillet over medium high heat. Add the ham strips, and brown on both sides; this may have to be done in batches. Remove the ham from the pan, and set aside.

2. Add the onion, garlic, and green pepper to the skillet, and sauté over medium heat for 3 minutes. Add the tomatoes, wine, thyme, and parsley to the pan. Bring to a boil, and season with cayenne pepper to taste.

3. Return the ham to the pan, and simmer the ham and vegetables, covered, over medium heat for 10 minutes. Remove the cover, and cook for an additional 5 minutes over medium high heat, stirring occasionally. Season with salt and additional cayenne pepper to taste.

4. Place a portion of rice on one edge of each tortilla, leaving a 2-inch margin on both sides. Arrange the ham and vegetables over the rice. Tuck in the sides to enclose the filling, and roll the tortillas firmly but gently, beginning with the filled side. Cut in half, and serve immediately.

NOTE: If using pita bread, place them flat on a counter, and spoon in a portion of rice. Arrange the ham slices and vegetables on top of the rice, and serve immediately. The ham mixture and rice can be prepared up to 2 days in advance and refrigerated, tightly covered. Reheat in a microwave oven or over low heat in a skillet.

Hands-On Chopped Tomatoes

To "chop" canned tomatoes, drain and put them in a mixing bowl, then crush them with your hands.

Pesto Melt

It takes longer to preheat the oven than it does to assemble this easy and delicious dish. The garlic and basil in the pesto transfer all their goodness to the other ingredients. These wraps can also be served at room temperature—perfect for a picnic. *Serves 6*

SUGGESTED WRAPPERS: Eight-inch flour tortillas ◎ Armenian lavash

Vegetable oil spray
¹/₂ cup pesto sauce
3 red bell peppers, roasted, peeled, seeded, and sliced; or 3 jarred roasted red bell peppers

4 plum tomatoes, cored, seeded, and thinly sliced
2 cups packed, stemmed and rinsed fresh arugula leaves
1¹/₂ cups grated mozzarella

1. Preheat the oven to 450°F. Cover a baking sheet with heavy-duty aluminum foil. Spray the foil with vegetable oil spray.

2. Spread 1 heaping tablespoon pesto sauce on half of each wrapper, leaving a 1¹/₂-inch margin on both sides. Layer the bell peppers, tomatoes, and arugula on top of the pesto, and sprinkle with the cheese. Tuck in the sides to enclose the filling, and roll wrappers firmly but gently, beginning with the filled edge. Place the rolls on the baking sheet, seam side down, and spray with oil.

3. Bake in the preheated oven for 5 minutes. Turn the rolls gently with a spatula, and bake an additional 4 to 5 minutes, or until browned. Allow to sit for 2 minutes, cut in half, and serve immediately.

NOTE: These can be assembled up to 1 day in advance and refrigerated, tightly covered.

Sweet and Sour Curried Vegetables with Basmati Rice

This wrap is easy to make, delicious, and versatile. Not only does it call for vegetables that are available year round, but it can be served hot or cold. Mixing the rice into the vegetables turns the dish into a great salad to serve at any meal. *Serves 6*

SUGGESTED WRAPPERS: Pita bread ◎ eight-inch flour tortillas

2 tablespoons vegetable oil
1 large onion, peeled and diced
2 garlic cloves, peeled and minced
1 1/2 pounds zucchini, trimmed and cut
   into 1/4-inch slices
1 red bell pepper, seeds and ribs
   removed, cut into 1/4-inch slices

1 to 2 tablespoons curry powder
1/2 cup chicken stock or water
1/3 cup sugar
1/4 cup freshly squeezed lemon juice
Salt and freshly ground black pepper
2 cups cooked basmati rice, hot (cool
   rice if serving dish cold)

1. Heat the oil in a large skillet over medium high heat. Add the onion and garlic, and sauté, stirring frequently, for 3 minutes until the onion is translucent. Add the zucchini and bell pepper to the pan, and sauté for an additional 3 minutes. Stir the curry powder into the vegetables, and cook for 1 minute.

2. Add the chicken stock, sugar, and lemon juice to the pan, and stir well. Cook over medium high heat for 5 minutes, or until the liquid is reduced by half and the vegetables are cooked but not mushy. Season with salt and pepper to taste. Either proceed to roll the filling or place the vegetables in a sealed container and refrigerate until cold.

3. Place a portion of rice inside the pocket of each pita, and top with a portion of vegetables. Serve immediately.

NOTE: If using tortillas, place a portion of rice along one edge of the tortilla, leaving a 1½-inch margin at both sides. Top the rice with the vegetables, tuck in the sides to enclose the filling, and roll tortillas firmly but gently, beginning with the filled edge. Cut in half on the diagonal, and serve immediately.

Grilled Wild Mushrooms with Herbed Tomato Sauce

Woodsy, earthy wild mushrooms are grilled or broiled, then bathed in spicy tomato sauce and sprinkled with Parmesan. This wrap can be made in minutes if you use jarred spaghetti sauce instead of the tomato sauce. *Serves 6*

SUGGESTED WRAPPERS: Pita bread ◎ Armenian lavash ◎ eight-inch flour tortillas

⅓ cup olive oil, divided
1 cup finely chopped onion
3 garlic cloves, peeled and minced
Two 1-pound cans peeled plum
    tomatoes, drained and chopped
½ cup dry red wine
¼ cup chopped fresh parsley

2 tablespoons chopped fresh basil
1 tablespoon chopped fresh thyme
Salt and freshly ground black pepper
30 to 36 large fresh shiitake mushroom
    caps, stemmed and wiped with a
    damp paper towel
⅓ to ½ cup freshly grated Parmesan

1. Heat 2 tablespoons oil in a medium saucepan over medium heat. Add the onion and garlic, and sauté for 3 minutes, stirring frequently, or until the onions are translucent. Add the tomatoes, wine, parsley, basil, and thyme. Bring to a boil over medium high heat, reduce the heat to medium, and cook the sauce for 20 minutes, stirring occasionally, or until it is reduced by half. Season with salt and pepper to taste, and keep warm.

2. While the sauce is cooking, light a charcoal or gas grill, or preheat the oven broiler. Brush the mushroom caps with the remaining oil, and sprinkle with salt and pepper to taste. Grill or broil the mushroom caps until brown and soft, about 2 minutes per side.

3. Spoon some of the sauce into each pita bread, and insert the mushrooms. Top with more sauce and a sprinkling of cheese. Serve immediately.

NOTE: If using lavash or flour tortillas, spoon some sauce onto one edge of each wrapper, leaving a 2-inch margin at one side. Arrange the mushrooms on top of the sauce, and top with more sauce and the cheese. Tuck the sides of the wrapper over the filling, and roll the wrappers firmly but gently, beginning with the filled side. Serve immediately. The tomato sauce can be made up to 2 days in advance and refrigerated, tightly covered; any leftover sauce can be frozen for up to 3 months.

Storing Wild Mushrooms

Store wild mushrooms, such as shiitakes, in paper bags. Plastic bags cause mushrooms to become moist and soggy. Another trick is to line a bowl with a cloth or paper towel, add the mushrooms, and cover with another cloth. Mushrooms keep up to a week stored this way.

Grilled Summer Vegetables with Provolone

Vegetables cooked on the grill become imbued with a haunting smoky flavor. Enlivened with herbs and provolone, this wrap becomes a memorable meal. *Serves 6*

SUGGESTED WRAPPERS: Ten-inch flour tortillas ◉ Armenian lavash

1/2 cup olive oil
1 tablespoon dried Italian seasoning
2 tablespoons crushed garlic
2 summer squash or zucchini (or 1 of each), trimmed and cut on the diagonal into 1/2-inch slices
1 large red onion, peeled and cut into 1/2-inch slices
1 large eggplant, peeled and cut into 1/2-inch slices

12 large mushroom caps, wiped with a damp paper towel
2 red or green bell peppers, seeds and ribs removed, cut into 1-inch wedges
6 plum tomatoes, cored and halved
Salt and freshly ground black pepper
1/2 pound provolone, grated

1. Light a charcoal or gas grill. Combine the olive oil with the Italian seasoning and garlic, and stir well. When the charcoal is covered with white ash, or the gas grill is preheated, brush the vegetable slices liberally with the oil mixture.

2. Grill the vegetables, turning as necessary with tongs, and brush liberally with the oil as they grill. The eggplant and mushrooms should be cooked to the point of softness, while the summer squash, onion, bell peppers, and tomatoes should retain their shape and texture. As the vegetables are cooked, remove them with tongs to a platter, and keep warm. Sprinkle the vegetables with salt and pepper to taste.

3. Place a portion of each vegetable in a line on one edge of each wrapper, leaving a 2-inch margin at both sides. Sprinkle the cheese over the vegetables, and tuck in the sides. Roll each wrapper firmly but gently, and keep the rolls tightly closed with toothpicks or metal skewers.

4. Brush the rolls with the seasoned oil, and place them on the grill, turning them gently with tongs until they are lightly browned. Remove them from the grill, cut each in half on the diagonal, and serve immediately.

NOTE: There are many combinations of vegetables that can be used for this dish: whole trimmed scallions, wild mushroom caps, sweet Vidalia onions, bell peppers of any color, and parboiled potato slices.

Microwaved Bacon

To cook bacon in the microwave oven, line a microwave-safe plate with two layers of paper towels. Put two strips of bacon on top. Cover with one paper towel, then two bacon strips. Finish with two paper towels. Cook on HIGH (100%) until crisp; the amount of time depends on the power of the oven.

Wraps Around the World

The difference between the recipes in this chapter and those in the previous one is that the ones here are closely linked to specific dishes from different cultures, and they are best suited to only one wrapper.

All Asian cuisines have food in wrappers, ranging from crispy rice paper pancakes to vegetable leaves and bread doughs. While I have based these wraps on authentic recipes, I've used some latitude in making them more "user-friendly" for today's busy cooks.

For example rather than frying Chinese shrimp toast or Vietnamese spring rolls *(cha gio)* in deep fat, I've devised methods for baking them. This decreases the amount of time needed to monitor the cooking as well as the amount of fat in the finished dish.

Also, traditional dishes from one culture have been merged with wrappers from another cuisine. Shanghai Burritos, for example, contain the filling of a Chinese egg roll, wrapped in Hispanic flour tortillas and baked until crisp. Muffuletta Quesadillas resemble the time-honored Creole sandwich born in New Orleans, but now the cold cuts and zesty olive salad are baked.

Another of today's food trends is the return to a formal fruit-and-cheese course in some of our country's haute-cuisine restaurants. Fruit and cheese are delicious served as wraps; try making Stilton, Pear, and Walnut Quesadillas, and other cheese and fruit combinations.

Mock Mu Shu Chicken

Flour tortillas are a great stand-in for the labor-intensive pancakes that are traditionally served with *mu shu* dishes in Chinese restaurants. *Serves 6*

1 pound boneless, skinless chicken
    breasts, cut into thin slivers
1/4 cup soy sauce
1 tablespoon dry sherry
2 tablespoons cornstarch
8 large dried shiitake mushrooms
1 ounce dried cloud-ear mushrooms
2 tablespoons vegetable oil

1/2 cup thinly sliced scallions, white
    parts and 4 inches of green tops
3 garlic cloves, peeled and minced
5 eggs, lightly beaten
Salt and freshly ground black pepper
1/2 cup plum sauce
Twelve 6-inch flour tortillas

1. Place the chicken in a mixing bowl. Combine the soy sauce, sherry, and cornstarch in a small cup, and pour the mixture over the chicken. Toss to coat well, and allow to sit at room temperature for 20 minutes.

2. While the chicken is marinating, pour boiling water over the shiitake and cloud-ear mushrooms, keeping them submerged with the back of a spoon. Allow them to rehydrate for 15 minutes, then drain, squeezing out extra moisture with your hands. Discard the stems, and thinly slice the mushrooms. Set aside.

3. Heat the oil in a large skillet or wok over medium high heat. Add the scallions and garlic, and stir-fry for 30 seconds. Add the chicken, and stir-fry for 2 minutes, or until the chicken is no longer pink. Add the mushrooms and eggs to the pan, and stir. Cook for 1 minute, then scrape the bottom of the pan to dislodge the cooked eggs. Cook for another 1 to 2 minutes, or until the eggs are just set. Season with salt and pepper to taste.

4. Spread plum sauce on the surface of each tortilla, and place some of the chicken mixture in a line in the center. Tuck one edge over the filling, and roll tortillas tightly but firmly to enclose the filling. Serve immediately.

NOTE: The recipe can also be made with pork tenderloin.

Baked Shrimp Toast Rolls

Chinese shrimp toasts are usually fried morsels of delicate shrimp combined with crunchy bread and water chestnuts. Here, the filling is wrapped and baked in white bread rolls rather than deep-fried. *Makes 12 rolls, or 24 to 36 pieces*

Vegetable oil spray
¾ pound shrimp, peeled and deveined
2 tablespoons chopped fresh ginger
1 tablespoon sesame oil
1 egg white
1 tablespoon dry sherry
2 tablespoons cornstarch

1 tablespoon soy sauce
2 scallions, trimmed, white parts and 3
    inches of green tops
⅓ cup chopped water chestnuts
Salt and freshly ground black pepper
12 slices white bread, trimmed and
    rolled (page 9)

1. Preheat the oven to 425°F. Cover a baking sheet with heavy-duty aluminum foil, and spray the foil with vegetable oil spray.

2. Place the shrimp in the work bowl of a food processor fitted with the steel blade along with the ginger, sesame oil, egg white, sherry, cornstarch, and soy sauce. Puree until smooth, scraping the sides of the bowl as necessary. Add the scallions, and pulse to chop and combine. Scrape the mixture into a bowl, and stir in the chopped water chestnuts. Season with salt and pepper to taste.

3. Spread the bread slices out on a counter, and place 1 heaping tablespoon of filling in a line across the long side of the bread. Roll the bread around the filling so that the edges meet, and place the rolls, seam side down, on the prepared baking sheet. Make all the rolls, and spray the tops with vegetable oil spray.

4. Bake for 5 minutes, then remove the baking sheet from the oven and turn the rolls over, seam side up, using a spatula. Bake for an additional 3 minutes. Cut the rolls into halves or thirds with a sharp serrated knife, and serve immediately or at room temperature.

NOTE: The filling can be prepared 1 day in advance and refrigerated, with a sheet of plastic wrap pressed into the surface. Roll and bake just prior to serving.

Asian-Style Beef and Barley Lettuce Cups

The nutty flavor of barley works very well with Asian seasoning. These can be served hot or at room temperature as an appetizer or a light entrée. *Serves 6*

½ cup pearl barley
½ cup soy sauce, divided
¼ cup sesame oil, divided
1 pound lean ground beef
1 teaspoon hot chile oil
1 tablespoon minced garlic
2 teaspoons finely minced ginger

4 scallions, white parts and 5 inches of green tops, trimmed and thinly sliced
1 teaspoon cornstarch
1 cup fresh bean sprouts, rinsed
Salt and freshly ground black pepper
12 to 18 large Boston or iceberg lettuce cups

1. Bring a pot of lightly salted water to a boil. Rinse the barley in a sieve under cold running water until the water is clear. Add the barley to the boiling water, and simmer uncovered for 25 to 30 minutes, or until it is tender but still chewy. Drain well, toss the barley with the half the soy sauce and half the sesame oil, and set aside.

2. Heat a wok or large skillet over medium high heat. Add the beef, and fry it for 3 minutes, breaking up lumps. Add the chile oil, garlic, ginger, and scallions, and stir-fry for 2 to 3 minutes, or until the beef is browned.

3. Mix the cornstarch with ⅓ cup cold water. Stir it into the beef mixture, along with the remaining soy sauce and sesame oil, and cook over low heat, stirring frequently, for 1 minute, or until lightly thickened. Add the bean sprouts and cooked barley, and cook for 1 to 2 minutes until the bean sprouts and barley are hot.

4. Place a portion of the mixture in the center of each lettuce cup, and tuck the sides and both edges around the filling. Serve immediately.

NOTE: Short-grain Japanese rice can be used in place of the barley. The dish can be prepared up to adding the bean sprouts and cooked barley up to 1 day in advance and refrigerated, tightly covered. Reheat it over a low flame or in a microwave oven.

Chicken in Lettuce Cups

Small portions of stir-fried foods wrapped in vegetable leaves are an authentic part of many Asian cuisines. The lettuce leaves form a textural contrast to the velvety chicken as well as encasing it. *Serves 6*

1 pound boneless, skinless chicken
    breasts, cut into 1½-inch cubes
2 tablespoons sesame oil
1 tablespoon minced garlic
1 tablespoon minced ginger
6 scallions, trimmed, white parts and 4
    inches of green tops, thinly sliced
One 8-ounce can water chestnuts,
    drained and chopped

¼ cup soy sauce
2 tablespoons hoisin sauce
1 tablespoon cider vinegar
1 teaspoon cornstarch
Salt and freshly ground black pepper
12 Boston or iceberg lettuce-leaf cups
1 ounce rice noodles, fried until crisp,
    for garnish (optional)

1. Place the chicken on a sheet of plastic wrap, and put it in the freezer for 15 minutes. Place the chicken in the work bowl of a food processor fitted with the steel blade, and chop coarsely, using an on-and-off pulsing action.

2. Heat the sesame oil in a large skillet over medium high heat. Add the garlic, ginger, and ³/₄ of the scallions. Stir-fry for 30 seconds. Add the chicken, and stir-fry for 3 to 4 minutes, breaking up the lumps, or until the chicken is no longer pink and is beginning to brown. Stir in the water chestnuts, and stir-fry for 1 minute.

3. Mix the soy sauce, hoisin sauce, vinegar, and cornstarch in a small bowl with ¼ cup cold water. Add it to the pan, and when the mixture boils and thickens, reduce the heat to low and simmer for 1 minute, stirring frequently. Season with salt and pepper to taste.

4. Spoon the mixture into the lettuce cups, garnish with the remaining scallion slices and fried rice noodles, if used. Serve immediately.

NOTE: Chow mein noodles, available at any supermarket, can be used instead of rice noodles. The chicken mixture can be prepared up to a day in advance and refrigerated, tightly covered with plastic wrap. Reheat in a microwave oven or over low heat before serving.

Steamed Chinese Dumplings

Watching carts with metal pans filled with steamed and fried *dim sum* wheeled through the aisles of a Chinese restaurant is a sensual delight, and one of my favorite foods from those carts are the steamed buns. After much experimentation, I discovered that using refrigerated biscuit dough produces similar results, but in less time than it takes to make a dough from scratch. *Makes 20*

Two 7½-ounce packages refrigerated home-style biscuit dough (not buttermilk)

1 recipe of any filling given below, well chilled

1. Cut parchment paper or waxed paper into twenty 2-inch squares. Separate the dough into individual portions; each circle will be approximately 2 inches in diameter. Place one dough section on a plate, and press the edge of the circle, leaving the center portion its original thickness, until it is 3½-inches in diameter.

2. Place a scant tablespoon of filling in the center of each circle. Using your fin-

Wraps Around the World

gers, gather the edges around the filling, and seal the dumplings closed by pinching the dough. Place the dumpling, seam side down, on a square of parchment paper, and shape the dumpling into a round ball. Place the dumpling on a bamboo steamer rack, and repeat with the remaining dough sections. Each 10-inch steamer rack holds 7 dumplings. If you don't have a bamboo steamer, one can be improvised. Place a cake rack on heatproof custard cups in the bottom of a stockpot. Since the rack and cups will not be as stable as a bamboo steamer, steam only one level of dumplings at a time.

3. Pour ½ inch of water into the bottom of a large stockpot, and when it comes to a boil, place a heat-proof custard cup in the pan and stack the bamboo steamers into the pot. Cover the pot, and steam for 10 minutes. Turn off the heat, and gently lift the cover away from you. Remove the steamer racks from the pan with tongs, and serve dumplings immediately.

NOTE: The fillings can be prepared up to 2 days in advance and refrigerated, tightly covered. The dumplings can be prepared for steaming up to 2 hours in advance and refrigerated. Do not steam the dumplings until just prior to serving.

Barbecued Pork Filling

¾ pound ground pork	1 tablespoon minced garlic
1 tablespoon dry sherry	¼ cup ketchup
¼ cup soy sauce, divided	¼ cup firmly packed light brown sugar
2 tablespoons vegetable oil	1 tablespoon white wine vinegar
½ cup finely chopped scallions, white parts and 4 inches of green tops	1 tablespoon sesame oil
	Salt and freshly ground black pepper

1. Combine the pork, sherry, and 2 tablespoons soy sauce in a mixing bowl, and marinate for 10 minutes.

2. Heat the vegetable oil in a wok or medium skillet over medium high heat. Add the scallions and garlic, and stir-fry for 30 seconds. Add the pork to the pan, breaking up the lumps, and cook for 4 to 5 minutes, or until the meat is no longer pink. Add the remaining soy sauce, ketchup, brown sugar, and vinegar to the pan, and bring to a boil. Reduce the heat to low, and simmer the mixture, stirring occasionally, for 15 minutes, or until it has thickened. Remove the pan from the heat, stir in the sesame oil, and season with salt and pepper to taste.

3. Spread the mixture in a shallow pan, press a sheet of plastic wrap directly into the top, and chill until filling is cold. Shape and steam the dumplings as described on page 91.

Chicken and Shiitake Mushroom Filling

3/4 pound boneless, skinless chicken
    breasts, cut into 1 1/2-inch cubes
1/3 cup oyster sauce, divided
1/2 teaspoon dried red pepper flakes
1 1/2 tablespoons cornstarch, divided
3 tablespoons vegetable oil
1 tablespoon finely minced fresh ginger

1 tablespoon finely minced garlic
1/3 cup chopped scallions, white parts
    and 4 inches of green tops
1/2 cup chopped fresh shiitake
    mushrooms
2 tablespoons soy sauce
Salt and freshly ground black pepper

1. Arrange chicken pieces on a baking sheet lined with plastic wrap, and place in the freezer for 15 minutes. Remove the chicken from the freezer, and chop it coarsely in a food processor fitted with the steel blade, using an on-and-off pulsing action.

2. Scrape the chicken into a mixing bowl, and add 2 tablespoons oyster sauce, red pepper flakes, and 2 teaspoons cornstarch. Mix well, and set aside to marinate for 10 minutes.

3. Heat the oil in a wok or large skillet over medium high heat. Add the ginger, garlic, and scallions, and stir-fry for 30 seconds. Add the mushrooms, and stir-fry for 1 minute. Add the chicken, and stir-fry for 2 to 3 minutes, or until the chicken has lost all its pink color.

4. Add the remaining oyster sauce and soy sauce to the pan along with 1/3 cup water. Bring to a boil, reduce the heat, and simmer over low heat for 2 minutes. Combine the remaining cornstarch with 2 tablespoons cold water. Add it to the pan,

and stir it into the mixture. Simmer for 1 minute, or until thickened. Season with salt and pepper to taste.

5. Spread the mixture in a shallow pan, press a sheet of plastic wrap directly into the top, and chill until the filling is cold. Shape and steam the dumplings as described on page 91.

Peking Pork Roll Ups

Flavorful pork sausage and crunchy bean sprouts and water chestnuts in a sweetened mustard sauce are inspired by the tastes and textures of Asian dishes. These wraps are so easy to make, and for parties, I cut them into 1-inch sections. *Serves 6*

1 pound ground pork
10 scallions, trimmed and thinly sliced, white parts and 6 inches of the green tops, divided
3 tablespoons finely chopped fresh ginger
3 tablespoons chopped fresh cilantro leaves
1 tablespoon minced garlic

2 tablespoons soy sauce
1 tablespoon dry sherry
1/2 cup finely diced water chestnuts
1/3 cup Dijon mustard
1/4 cup hoisin sauce
Six 8-inch flour tortillas
1 1/2 cups fresh bean sprouts or thinly sliced bok choy
Salt and freshly ground black pepper

1. Preheat the oven to 375°F. Line a 9 × 13-inch baking pan with heavy-duty aluminum foil.

2. Combine the pork with half the scallions, ginger, cilantro, garlic, soy sauce, sherry, and water chestnuts. Mix well to combine. Form the mixture into a log 12 inches long and 2 inches wide in the baking pan. Bake the pork in the preheated oven for 25 minutes, or until the top has browned and the meat registers 160°F. on a meat thermometer. Remove the pork from the oven, cut into 12 slices, and keep warm. Mix the mustard and hoisin sauce, and set aside.

3. Lay the tortillas out on a counter, and spread some of the mustard sauce on half of each tortilla, leaving a 1½-inch margin on both sides. Place 2 slices of pork in the center, and place some bean sprouts and the remaining scallions over the meat. Tuck in the ends to enclose the filling, and roll the tortillas firmly but gently, beginning with the filled edge. Cut in half on the diagonal, and serve immediately.

NOTE: The meat can be prepared up to 2 days in advance and refrigerated, tightly covered. Heat it to at least room temperature before wrapping.

Shanghai Burritos

Talk about fusion food! A Chinese spring roll filling is wrapped and baked crispy in Hispanic flour tortillas rather than deep-fried in egg roll wrappers. In place of ground pork, substitute cooked chicken or beef. *Serves 6*

6 large dried shiitake mushrooms
Vegetable oil spray
¼ cup vegetable oil
2 tablespoons minced garlic
½ cup chopped scallions, white parts
    and 4 inches of green tops
½ pound ground pork
4 cups shredded green cabbage

½ pound tiny cooked shrimp
    (sometimes called salad shrimp)
1 cup fresh bean sprouts, rinsed
¼ cup soy sauce
2 tablespoons sesame oil
Salt and freshly ground black pepper
Six 8-inch flour tortillas

1. Place the mushrooms in a small mixing bowl, and cover them with very hot tap water, pressing them into the water with the back of a spoon. Allow them to rehy-

drate for 30 minutes, then remove them from the water, squeeze them to extract as much water as possible, cut off and discard the stems, and coarsely chop the caps. Set aside.

2. Preheat the oven to 450°F. Cover a baking sheet with heavy-duty aluminum foil, and spray the foil with oil.

3. Heat the vegetable oil in a wok or large skillet over medium high heat. Add the garlic and scallions, and stir-fry for 30 seconds. Add the pork, and stir-fry for 2 minutes, breaking up any lumps. Add the cabbage, and stir-fry for 2 minutes. Add ⅓ cup water to the pan along with the reserved mushrooms. Stir well, raise the heat to high, cover the pan, and cook for 2 minutes.

4. Remove the pan from the heat, and stir in the shrimp, bean sprouts, soy sauce, and sesame oil. Season with salt and pepper to taste.

5. Lay the tortillas on a counter, and place a portion of filling on one edge of each, leaving a 1½-inch margin on both sides. Tuck the sides over the filling, and then roll the tortillas firmly but gently, beginning with the filled side. Place the rolls, seam side down, on the baking sheet. Spray the rolls with oil, and bake in the preheated oven for 5 minutes. Turn the rolls gently with tongs, and bake an additional 5 to 7 minutes, or until crisp. Remove the rolls from the oven, cut in half on the diagonal, and serve immediately.

NOTE: The filling can be prepared for baking up to 1 day in advance and refrigerated, tightly covered. Allow it to reach room temperature before baking.

Vietnamese Spring Rolls

~~~~

These *cha gio,* crispy Vietnamese spring rolls wrapped in rice paper, are baked instead of fried, making them much lighter and quicker to prepare. While these have ground pork as the basis for the filling, ground turkey or chicken can be substituted. *Makes 18 rolls*

5 large dried shiitake mushrooms
1 ounce bean thread noodles (see Note)
Vegetable oil spray
1/2 pound ground pork
1 cup fresh bean sprouts, rinsed and cut into 1-inch lengths
1/2 cup shredded carrot
1/2 cup chopped scallions, white parts and 4 inches of green tops

2 tablespoons minced garlic
3 tablespoons Vietnamese fish sauce
2 large eggs, lightly beaten
1 teaspoon sugar
Salt and freshly ground black pepper
1/2 cup sugar
18 rice paper pancakes

1. Soak the dried mushrooms and bean thread noodles in separate bowls of very hot tap water for 30 minutes. Remove the mushrooms, and squeeze well to extract as much water as possible. Discard the stems, and finely chop the mushrooms. Drain the bean thread noodles in a sieve. Place them on a cutting board in a long log shape, and cut into 1-inch pieces. Measure out 1/2 cup noodles, and discard the rest.

2. Preheat the oven to 450°F. Cover a baking sheet with heavy-duty aluminum foil, and spray the foil with vegetable oil spray. Place the mushrooms and noodles in a mixing bowl, and add the pork, bean sprouts, carrot, scallions, garlic, fish sauce, eggs, sugar, and salt and pepper to taste. You will need very little salt, since the fish sauce is salty. Mix well to combine.

3. Fill a wide mixing bowl with very hot tap water, and stir in the sugar until it is dissolved. Place a damp tea towel in front of you on the counter. Place the rice paper pancakes on a plate, and cover with a barely damp towel.

4. Fill one rice paper pancake at a time, keeping the remainder covered. Totally immerse the pancake in hot water for 2 seconds. Remove it and place it on the damp tea towel; it will become pliable within a few seconds. Gently fold the front edge of the pancake ⅓ of the way to the top. Lightly spray the unfilled pancake with vegetable oil spray. Place about 2 tablespoons of the filling on the folded-up portion, and shape it into a log, leaving a 2-inch margin on each side. Fold the sides of the pancake over the filling, and roll tightly but gently, beginning with the filled side. Place the roll on the baking sheet, seam side down, and continue to fill the rice paper pancakes in the same manner.

5. Spray the tops and sides of the rolls with vegetable oil spray, and place them in the center of the preheated oven. Bake for 12 minutes, then turn the rolls gently with tongs, and bake for an additional 10 to 12 minutes, or until the rolls are browned. Remove the pan from the oven, and blot the rolls with paper towels. Slice each in half on the diagonal, and serve immediately.

NOTE: Bean thread noodles, also called "cellophane noodles," are found in the Asian section of most supermarkets, and in Asian groceries. The filling for the spring rolls can be prepared up to 1 day in advance and refrigerated, tightly covered. The rolls can be baked up to 2 days in advance and refrigerated, tightly covered. Reheat in a 400°F. oven for 5 to 7 minutes.

Stilton, Pear, and Walnut Quesadillas

Port wine is usually paired with sharp Stilton cheese and often accompanied by a bowl of walnuts and ripe pears. These same ingredients can be combined in a quesadilla and enjoyed as a wrap. Serve with a mixed green salad for lunch or a light supper. *Serves 6*

2 ripe pears, peeled, cored, and thinly sliced
⅔ cup port
Six 6-inch flour tortillas

½ pound Stilton, crumbled
⅔ cup chopped walnuts, toasted
Vegetable oil spray or melted butter

1. Place the pear slices in a heavy resealable plastic bag, and add the port. Close the bag, and allow the pears to marinate for at least 1 hour at room temperature.

2. Preheat the oven to 450°F. Cover a baking sheet with heavy-duty aluminum foil. Spray the sheet with oil or brush it with melted butter. Arrange the tortillas so that they are half on the baking sheet.

3. Divide the cheese among the tortillas, covering only the half of each tortilla resting on the baking sheet. Drain the pears and layer them on top of the cheese, and then sprinkle with the chopped nuts. Fold the untreated half of the tortilla over the filling, and press gently with the palm of your hand or a spatula to seal it closed.

4. Evenly space the quesadillas on the prepared baking sheet, and spray or brush the tops with oil or butter. Bake in the preheated oven for 5 minutes. Turn the quesadillas gently, and then bake for an additional 4 to 5 minutes, or until brown and crisp. Allow them to sit for 2 minutes, and then cut each in half and serve immediately.

NOTE: The quesadillas can be prepared for baking up to 3 hours in advance and kept at room temperature.

Muffuletta Quesadillas

The muffuletta is the classic Creole-Italian hero sandwich, which originated at the Central Grocery in New Orleans. The traditional sandwich consists of layered cold cuts and cheese on a thick round roll. For a southwestern-Louisiana wrap, the same ingredients are layered with a pickled-olive salad inside tortillas and heated. *Serves 6*

Vegetable oil spray
³/₄ cup olive salad, drained and chopped
2 teaspoons minced garlic
1 tablespoon chopped fresh parsley
Six 6-inch flour tortillas

6 slices mortadella, about ¹/₄ pound
6 slices baked ham, about ¹/₄ pound
12 slices Genoa salami, about ¹/₄ pound
6 slices provolone, about ¹/₄ pound

1. Preheat the oven to 450°F. Cover a baking sheet with heavy-duty aluminum foil, and spray with vegetable oil spray. Combine the chopped olive salad, garlic, and parsley in a small bowl, and set aside.

2. Place the tortillas so that they are half on the baking sheet, and layer the mortadella, ham, salami, and provolone on the half of each circle resting on the baking sheet. Top the cheese with 1 heaping tablespoon olive salad, and then fold the tortillas over the filling, and press closed with the palm of your hand or a spatula. Space the quesadillas evenly on the baking sheet.

3. Spray the tops of the quesadillas with vegetable oil spray. Bake in the center of the preheated oven for 5 minutes. Turn gently with a spatula, pressing them down if the top has separated from the filling. Return them to the oven for an additional 5 minutes, or until browned. Allow to sit for 3 minutes, then cut each in half, and serve immediately.

NOTE: The quesadillas can be assembled up to a day in advance. Refrigerate them in layers separated by a layer of plastic wrap. Spray with oil and cook just before serving.

Cuban Roll Ups

The Cuban sandwich, or *medianoche* as it is called in Miami, is a combination of full-flavored meats and cheese spruced up with crunchy dill pickles. This wrapped version retains all those qualities, and is easier to assemble and eat. *Serves 6*

Vegetable oil spray
Six 8-inch flour tortillas
4 tablespoons (½ stick) unsalted butter,
   softened

½ pound Swiss cheese, shredded
½ pound roast pork, thinly sliced
¾ cup thinly sliced dill pickles
½ pound baked ham, thinly sliced

1. Preheat the oven to 450°F. Cover a baking sheet with heavy-duty aluminum foil, and spray the foil with vegetable oil spray.

2. Place the tortillas on a counter, and spread them with a thin layer of butter. Place a portion of cheese along one edge, leaving a 1½-inch margin on both sides. Layer the pork, pickles, and ham on top of the cheese. Tuck in the sides to enclose the filling, and roll the tortillas firmly but gently, beginning with the filled side. Place the tortillas, seam side down, on the baking sheet.

3. Spray the tops of the rolls with vegetable oil spray, and bake for 8 to 10 minutes, or until brown. Allow the rolls to sit for 2 minutes, then cut in half on the diagonal and serve immediately.

NOTE: The wraps can be prepared for baking up to 1 day in advance and refrigerated, tightly covered with plastic wrap. To bake, preheat the oven to 425°F., then bake for 10 to 12 minutes.

Santa Fe Chicken Quesadillas

These southwestern-style favorites are always a crowd pleaser at my parties. The strips of chicken are enhanced by a combination of spicy cheese and creamy mayonnaise. If you want to serve the quesadillas as hors d'oeuvres, use eight 6-inch tortillas to make 16 wedges. *Serves 6*

1½ **pounds boneless, skinless chicken breasts, pounded to an even** ½-**inch thickness and cut into** ½-**inch strips**
¾ **cup tomato salsa, divided**
Salt and freshly ground black pepper
¼ **cup mayonnaise**

2 **teaspoons chile powder**
Six 8-inch flour tortillas
3 **plum tomatoes, cored, seeded, and thinly sliced**
½ **pound Jalapeño Jack, grated**
Cilantro sprigs
Vegetable oil spray

1. Place the chicken in a resealable plastic bag, and add ¹/₂ cup tomato salsa along with salt and pepper to taste. Marinate the chicken at room temperature for 1 hour or overnight in the refrigerator.

2. Preheat the oven to 450°F. Line a 9 × 13-inch baking pan with heavy-duty aluminum foil. Remove the chicken from the marinade, and place the strips in one layer in the pan. Strain the marinade. Discard the liquid, and sprinkle the vegetables from it over the chicken. Bake the chicken for 15 minutes, turning the pieces with a slotted spatula after 10 minutes. Remove the chicken from the oven, and set aside. Mix the mayonnaise with the chile powder and the remaining ¹/₄ cup salsa, and set aside.

3. Cover 2 baking sheets with heavy-duty aluminum foil. Spray the foil with vegetable oil spray. Place tortillas so that they are half on the baking sheets, and divide the chicken among the halves resting on the baking sheets. Spread 1 heaping tablespoon chile mayonnaise on top of the chicken, and then add the tomato slices and sprinkle each tortilla with cheese. Press cilantro sprigs into the cheese, fold each tortilla in half, and press gently with the palm of your hand or a spatula to enclose the filling. Space the quesadillas evenly on the baking sheets. Spray the tops of the quesadillas with vegetable oil spray.

4. Bake the quesadillas in the preheated oven for 5 minutes. Turn carefully with a spatula, and bake an additional 5 minutes, or until browned. Wait 2 minutes, then cut the quesadillas in half and serve immediately.

NOTE: The chicken can be baked up to a day in advance and refrigerated, tightly covered with plastic wrap. Bring it to room temperature before assembling and baking the quesadillas.

Welsh Rarebit Quesadillas

Bubbly cheese on crisp toast with bacon and tomatoes is classic "pub grub" in England, but when wrapped in tortillas this dish becomes a grilled cheese with bacon and tomato wrap. *Serves 6*

**Vegetable oil spray or reserved bacon
    grease**
Six 6-inch flour tortillas
2 tablespoons Dijon mustard
2 cups grated sharp Cheddar

**1 pound bacon, cooked crisp and
    drained**
**3 plum tomatoes, cored, seeded, and
    thinly sliced**

1. Preheat the oven to 450°F. Cover a baking sheet with heavy-duty aluminum foil, and spray the foil with vegetable oil spray or brush it with bacon grease.

2. Place the prepared baking sheet on a counter, and arrange the tortillas so that they are half on the baking sheet. Spread 1 teaspoon mustard on each half, top the mustard with 1/3 cup grated cheese per tortilla, and then evenly divide the bacon and tomato slices. Fold the unfilled side of the tortilla over the filling, and press gently with the palm of your hand or a spatula to close tightly. Arrange the filled quesadillas so that they are evenly spaced on the baking sheet.

3. Spray the tops of the quesadillas with vegetable oil spray or brush them with bacon grease. Bake in the preheated oven for 5 minutes, then turn gently with a spatula, and bake for an additional 5 minutes, or until the quesadillas are nicely brown. Remove the quesadillas from the oven, and allow to rest for 2 minutes. Cut each in half and serve immediately.

NOTE: The quesadillas can be prepared for baking up to 3 hours in advance and kept at room temperature.

Peppered Pork Burritos

These wraps join traditional southwestern flavors with goat cheese and sun-dried tomatoes. Use chicken breasts in place of the peppery pork if you prefer. *Serves 6*

2 pounds pork tenderloin, trimmed of all fat and silver skin

Salt

3 tablespoons coarsely ground black pepper

4 ounces goat cheese, softened

Six 10-inch flour tortillas

1/2 cup finely slivered oil-packed sun-dried tomatoes

3/4 cup guacamole (purchased or page 26)

3 plum tomatoes, cored, seeded, and diced

1/2 red or yellow bell pepper, seeds and ribs removed, chopped

1 1/2 cups shredded iceberg or romaine lettuce

1. Preheat the oven to 450°F. Season the pork tenderloins with salt, and rub them with pepper. Place the pork on a rack in a shallow roasting pan, tucking the thin ends under so that the tenderloins are an even thickness. Roast for 15 to 20 minutes, or until brown and the meat registers 160°F. on a meat thermometer. Allow the pork to rest for 10 minutes, then dice it into 1/2-inch pieces.

2. Spread the goat cheese on half of each tortilla, leaving a 2-inch margin on both sides. Sprinkle the sun-dried tomatoes over the goat cheese, and spread 2 tablespoons guacamole in the center of each tortilla. Top the guacamole with diced pork, and then divide the plum tomatoes, chopped bell pepper, and lettuce on top.

3. To serve, tuck in the sides and fold one side of the tortilla firmly around the filling. Continue to roll, and then cut in half on the diagonal before serving.

NOTE: The pork can be roasted up to 2 days in advance and refrigerated, tightly covered. Warm it in a 250°F. oven or in a microwave oven before assembling the burritos.

Spicy Moroccan Chicken Turnovers

Every culture has its version of chicken pot pie, and one of my favorite ones is *bisteeya,* from Morocco. Traditionally a spicy chicken mixture with crunchy almonds and scrambled eggs, it is layered between sheets of phyllo dough, but the filling can be baked in pastry dough for individual wraps as well. This is a great way to stretch a roasted chicken into a second night's dinner. *Serves 6*

2 tablespoons olive oil
1 cup diced onion
3 teaspoons cinnamon
1 teaspoon turmeric
$1/2$ teaspoon dried ground ginger
4 large eggs, lightly beaten, divided
$1/3$ cup chicken stock or water
3 cups diced cooked chicken

$1/3$ cup chopped fresh parsley
$1/2$ cup slivered almonds, toasted
Salt and freshly ground black pepper
1 package refrigerated pie-crust sheets, at room temperature (or enough homemade dough for a double crust pie)

1. Preheat the oven to 400°F. Cover a baking sheet with heavy-duty aluminum foil.

2. Place the olive oil in a large skillet over medium heat. Add the onion and sauté, stirring frequently, for 5 minutes, or until the onion is almost soft. Add the cinnamon, turmeric, and ginger to the pan, and cook over low heat for 1 minute.

3. Combine 3/4 of the eggs with the stock, and add them to the pan. Cook over low heat until the eggs are about 3/4 cooked, stirring frequently. Stir the chicken, parsley, and almonds into the mixture, and remove the pan from the heat. Season with salt and pepper to taste.

4. Place 1 pie-crust sheet between 2 sheets of plastic wrap, and roll it into a 12-inch circle. Using a dish or pot lid as a guide, cut three 6-inch circles from the sheet. Repeat with the second sheet of pie crust. Place a portion of the filling on one side of each circle, leaving a 1/2-inch border. Fold the dough over the filling, and crimp the edges of the turnovers with the tines of a fork. Cut four ½-inch slits in the tops, and brush the tops with the remaining beaten eggs. Space the turnovers evenly on the baking sheet.

5. Bake the turnovers in the center of the preheated oven for 35 to 40 minutes, or until golden brown. Allow to sit for 5 minutes before serving; the turnovers can also be served at room temperature.

NOTE: The filling can be prepared up to 1 day in advance and refrigerated, tightly covered. Do not stir in the parsley or almonds until just prior to baking. Leftover turkey can be substituted for the chicken.

Vegetable and Cheese Calzone

Very little time is needed for cooking the calzone filling before the completed wraps bake unattended in the oven. This dish is delicious with salami or prosciutto; if adding either, omit salt. *Serves 6*

2 tablespoons olive oil
1 medium onion, peeled and diced
2 garlic cloves, peeled and minced
¼ pound green beans, stemmed and cut into ½-inch pieces
¼ pound thin asparagus, cut into ½-inch pieces (cut stems in half lengthwise if not thin)
1 cup fresh or frozen peas

One 1-pound can diced tomatoes, drained
2 tablespoons chopped fresh basil
Salt and freshly ground black pepper
1½ cups grated Italian Fontina or provolone
Pizza dough (homemade or purchased refrigerated)
Cornmeal

1. Preheat the oven to 450°F. Place a pizza stone or baking sheet in the oven to preheat.

2. Heat the olive oil in a large skillet over medium high heat. Add the onion and garlic, and sauté, stirring frequently, for 3 minutes. Add the green beans, asparagus, peas, and tomatoes, and cook for an additional 5 minutes, stirring often. Stir in the basil, and season with salt and pepper to taste.

3. Divide the pizza dough into 6 parts, and roll each into a 6-inch circle. Place a portion of vegetables on half of each circle, leaving a ½-inch margin around it. Divide the cheese on top of the vegetables, brush the edge of the calzone with water, and fold over the untreated dough. Press the edges together with the tines of a fork to seal in the filling. Sprinkle the hot baking sheet or pizza stone with cornmeal, and space the calzone evenly on the sheet.

4. Bake for 10 minutes, then reduce the oven temperature to 400°F., and bake for an additional 10 minutes, or until the crust is browned. Serve immediately.

NOTE: The vegetable mixture can be prepared 1 day in advance and refrigerated, tightly covered. Bring it to room temperature before stuffing and baking the calzone.

Gyros

Gyros, the ubiquitous Greek wrap of minced lamb and a tangy yogurt sauce rolled in lavash, can easily be created at home. *Serves 6*

1½ pounds ground lamb
2 tablespoons finely chopped shallots
2½ tablespoons minced garlic, divided
2 tablespoons chopped fresh basil
1 tablespoon chopped fresh thyme
2 teaspoons ground cumin
2 teaspoons chile powder
¼ cup chopped fresh parsley

⅓ cup Italian-flavored bread crumbs
Salt and freshly ground black pepper
1 cup yogurt cheese (page 5)
½ cup chopped tomato
½ cup chopped, peeled, and seeded cucumber
½ cup chopped onion
6 Armenian lavash

1. Preheat the oven to 400°F. Line the interior of a 10 × 15-inch jelly-roll pan with heavy-duty aluminum foil.

2. Combine the lamb, shallots, 2 tablespoons garlic, basil, thyme, cumin, chile powder, parsley, and bread crumbs in a mixing bowl, and mix well with your hands. Season with salt and pepper to taste, and form the meat mixture into a log the length of the baking sheet, and about 1½ inches high.

3. Bake the lamb mixture in the preheated oven for 20 minutes, or until browned. While the lamb is baking, combine the yogurt cheese, tomato, cucumber, onion, and remaining garlic in a medium mixing bowl. Season with salt and pepper, and allow it to stand at room temperature.

4. Remove the lamb from the oven, cut into 6 equal slices, and place each along one edge of a lavash, and spoon the sauce on top. Tuck the sides over to enclose the filling, and roll the lavash firmly but gently, beginning on the filled side. Cut in half on the diagonal, and serve immediately.

NOTE: The lamb and sauce can be prepared up to a day in advance and refrigerated, covered with plastic wrap. Reheat the lamb, covered in aluminum foil, in a 325°F. oven for 10 to 15 minutes, or until warmed through.

Separating Bacon

If packaged bacon slices are stuck together, roll up the entire package crosswise. Then unroll the package and all the bacon strips will separate easily. Or remove the bacon from the its wrapping and drop it all in one piece onto the griddle, under the broiler, or in the oven. The bacon will come unstuck as it cooks, and the melting fat acts as a lubricant.

Wrapping Up
Breakfast and Brunch

Studies have shown that when people skip a meal during the day, it's usually breakfast, and the reason given most often is lack of time to sit down and eat traditional
breakfast foods. While the recipes in this chapter do not include some magical way to
wrap up dried cereal with milk, there are a myriad of breakfast and brunch dishes that
lend themselves to wrapping.

Adding enticing additions to scrambled eggs, and then wrapping them in sturdy
pita bread before you leave the house is just one way to enjoy a nourishing breakfast
with little preparation.

Certain brunch wraps have southwestern flavors—spicy chorizo, Monterey Jack
with salsa, and oven-fried eggs. Quesadillas filled with succulent ham, apples, and
Cheddar cheese turn familiar lunch and dinner fare into a delectable breakfast/brunch
wrap.

You'll also find many other light yet flavorful breakfast and brunch foods, including quesadillas that join asparagus, hard-cooked eggs, ham, and Swiss cheese. And
there are several recipes for incorporating fresh fruit in this important first meal of
the day.

Spanish Omelet Wrap

~~~~~

In Spain, a tortilla is an omelet filled with a medley of wonderful ingredients, wrapped and eaten hot or at room temperature as a *tapa*. This great brunch wrap contains everything for a complete meal—eggs, sausage, ham, potatoes, and vegetables. *Serves 6*

SUGGESTED WRAPPERS: Eight-inch flour tortillas ◉ pita bread

2 medium red boiling potatoes, peeled and cut into 1/2-inch dice
1/4 cup olive oil, divided
1 large onion, peeled and diced
1/2 pound chorizo sausage, cut into 1/2-inch dice
1/4 pound Spanish cured ham, cut into 1/2-inch dice

One 4-ounce jar pimiento slices, drained
1/2 cup cooked peas
1/2 cup cooked green beans, cut into 1-inch pieces
2 plum tomatoes, cored, seeded, and finely diced
8 large eggs, well beaten
Salt and freshly ground black pepper

1. Bring a large pot of salted water to a boil. Add the potato cubes, and boil for 5 to 7 minutes, or until the potatoes are just tender. Drain, and set aside.

2. Heat 2 tablespoons olive oil in a large skillet over medium high heat. Add the potato cubes, and fry for 3 to 4 minutes, or until lightly brown. Remove the potatoes from the pan with a slotted spoon, and set aside. Add the remaining oil to the pan, and sauté the onion over medium heat for 3 to 5 minutes, or until translucent and beginning to soften. Add the chorizo and ham to the pan, and cook for 2 minutes. Add the pimiento, peas, green beans, and tomatoes to the pan, and stir well to combine. Stir the potato cubes back into the pan.

3. Season the eggs with salt and pepper to taste; use very little salt since the meats are salty. Add the eggs to the pan, and cook over medium heat until the eggs are set. Place a plate over the skillet, and invert the omelet on the plate. Slide the omelet back into the skillet to cook the other side.

4. Remove the pan from the heat, and cut the omelet into serving portions. Place the tortillas on a counter, and place a portion of omelet on one edge of each tortilla, leaving a 1¹/₂-inch margin on the sides. Tuck the sides over the filling, and wrap the omelet in the tortilla firmly but gently, beginning with the filled edge. Cut in half on the diagonal, and serve immediately.

NOTE: If using pita bread, cut the omelet into wedges, and insert one inside each pita pocket. The omelet filling can be prepared up to 1 day in advance and refrigerated, tightly covered. Reheat the filling over low heat before adding the eggs to the pan.

Nuevos Rancheros

Here's my version of *huevos rancheros*—with spicy sausage and creamy cheese right in the tortilla with the eggs and salsa. The level of spiciness depends on the heat of the chorizo used and the salsa. To make this for one or two people, fry the eggs in a nonstick skillet. To serve a crowd, baking the eggs in the oven ensures that everyone eats a hot dish at the same time. *Serves 6*

1 pound bulk chorizo sausage or 1
    pound chorizo links, skins
    removed, chopped
3 tablespoons unsalted butter
12 large eggs
Salt and freshly ground black pepper
Six 10-inch flour tortillas

1¹/₂ cups grated Monterey Jack
1 tablespoon sliced green olives
1¹/₂ cups tomato salsa, heated
Sour cream
Avocado slices (optional)
Chopped fresh cilantro leaves (optional)

1. Preheat the oven to 350°F. Cover 2 baking sheets with heavy-duty aluminum foil.

2. Place the chorizo in a large cold skillet over medium high heat. Cook the sausage, stirring frequently and breaking up any lumps, for 5 minutes, or until the sausage is browned. Remove the sausage from the pan with a slotted spoon, and set aside.

3. Place the butter in a glass or metal 9 × 13-inch baking pan, and place it in the preheated oven until the butter has melted. Remove the pan from the oven, and tilt it until the butter spreads all over the bottom and 2 inches up the sides of the pan. Break the eggs one by one into the baking pan, and sprinkle them with salt and pepper to taste. Bake the eggs for 5 to 7 minutes, or until the whites have cooked into a solid layer. Remove the pan from the oven, and with a knife separate the eggs into 12 sections. Turn the eggs gently with a spatula, and return the pan to the oven for an additional 2 to 4 minutes, depending on if you want the eggs well cooked or runny.

4. While the eggs are baking, place the tortillas on the prepared baking sheets, and sprinkle ¼ cup cheese on one half of each, leaving a 2-inch margin on both sides. Place the baking sheets in the oven for 3 to 4 minutes, or until the cheese has melted. Divide the chorizo on top of the cheese.

5. Place 2 cooked eggs in the center of each tortilla and top them with ¼ cup salsa. Top with sour cream, avocado slices, green olives, and cilantro, if desired. Tuck in the sides of the tortillas to enclose the filling, and roll the tortillas firmly but gently, beginning on the filled side. Serve immediately without cutting.

NOTE: The dish can also be made with scrambled or poached eggs.

Brunch Wraps

～～～

Here is a general method for wrapping up a basic scrambled egg dish along with a list of toppings to personalize the dish. An important benefit to wrapping food in sturdy flour tortillas or pita bread is that thick sauces and other additions can be used. *Serves 6*

SUGGESTED WRAPPERS: Ten-inch flour tortillas ◎ pita bread

12 large eggs
¹/₃ cup sour cream
¹/₄ cup heavy cream or milk
Salt and freshly ground black pepper

1¹/₂ cups topping (page 114); or other selection of your choice
4 tablespoons (¹/₂ stick) unsalted butter, sliced

   1. Break the eggs into a large mixing bowl, and add the sour cream, cream, and salt and pepper to taste. Whisk with a large balloon whisk until light and fluffy.

   2. Prepare desired topping.

   3. Heat a large skillet over medium heat, and add the butter. Tilt the skillet so that the butter covers the bottom and 2 inches up the sides of the pan. Lower the heat to low, pour in the eggs, and cover the pan. Cook the eggs for 3 minutes. Using a metal spatula, scrape the cooked eggs into the center of the pan. Re-cover the pan and repeat in 3 minutes. At this point the eggs should be about ³/₄ set. Stir, remove the pan from the heat, and allow to sit, covered, for 2 minutes. If grated cheese is part of the topping, sprinkle it over the eggs right before they are removed from the stove.

   4. Place the tortillas on a counter, and spoon a portion of scrambled eggs on one edge, leaving a 2-inch margin on both sides. Top the scrambled eggs with the prepared topping(s). Tuck in the sides, and roll the tortilla firmly but gently, beginning with the filled edge. Cut in half on the diagonal, and serve immediately.

NOTE: If using pita bread, spoon some of the topping into the bottom of the pocket, then spoon in the cooked eggs. End with more topping, pushing it down into the eggs, if appropriate.

BRUNCH WRAP TOPPINGS ◎ 1 pound bacon, cooked crisp and crumbled, mixed with 1 cup Alfredo sauce and ¼ cup finely diced tomato ◎ ½ cup each diced onion and red bell pepper, sautéed until soft in 2 tablespoons butter, and ½ cup diced ham ◎ 2 large potatoes, cut into ½-inch cubes and sautéed until crisp in ¼ cup olive oil, and ½ cup diced onion, sautéed in 2 tablespoons butter until soft and brown ◎ 3 tablespoons mixed fresh chopped herbs (parsley, thyme, oregano, rosemary and/or basil) added to the eggs, with 1 cup grated Swiss cheese and ½ cup chopped fresh tomato as toppings ◎ 1 cup mild or hot Italian sausage, fried until brown, mixed with ½ cup spaghetti sauce and ½ cup grated mozzarella ◎ ¼ pound fresh shiitake mushrooms, sautéed in 3 tablespoons unsalted butter, and 1 cup grated Gruyère ◎ ½ cup finely chopped sun-dried tomatoes packed in oil, ¼ cup diced Niçoise or Kalamata olives, and ½ cup sautéed onions ◎ ½ cup diced smoked salmon, 3 tablespoons minced chives, and ½ cup crème fraîche or sour cream ◎ One 10-ounce package frozen creamed spinach (prepared as directed), ½ cup diced ham, and ½ cup grated Swiss cheese ◎ ½ cup stir-fried asparagus, cut into ½-inch pieces, ½ cup sautéed wild mushrooms, and ½ cup grated smoked mozzarella ◎ ½ cup crumbled blue cheese mixed with ½ cup sour cream and 6 tablespoons red or black caviar ◎ 6 ounces crabmeat mixed with ½ cup tartar sauce; add ¼ cup chopped scallions to the eggs before scrambling them ◎ 1 cup sautéed diced salami and ½ cup sautéed onions ◎ Southwest Corn and Sausage Toss (page 70) ◎ Sauce from Grilled Shrimp with Leeks, Bacon, and Wild Mushrooms (page 45)

Corned Beef Hash and Fried Egg Burritos

There are few morning foods I love as much as homemade corned beef hash topped with a fried egg. A tortilla with corned beef from the deli department and leftover or refrigerated mashed potatoes make this usually time-consuming favorite a ready-in-minutes hearty breakfast or brunch treat. Since the hash can be prepared in advance, these wraps are perfect for a crowd. *Serves 6*

SUGGESTED WRAPPERS: Eight-inch flour tortillas ◎ Armenian lavash

3 tablespoons unsalted butter, divided
2 tablespoons vegetable oil
1 large sweet onion (such as Bermuda or Vidalia), peeled and chopped
1 red bell pepper, seeds and ribs removed, chopped
2 teaspoons minced garlic

1 pound cooked corned beef, coarsely chopped
2 cups mashed potatoes
1 teaspoon chopped fresh thyme
Salt and freshly ground black pepper
6 eggs

1. Preheat the oven to 350°F. Heat 1 tablespoon butter and the oil in a large skillet over medium heat. Add the onion, bell pepper, and garlic, and sauté, stirring frequently, for 10 minutes, or until the vegetables are soft. Add the corned beef, mashed potatoes, and thyme to the pan, and mix well. Season with salt and pepper to taste.

2. Place the remaining butter in a glass or metal 9 × 13-inch baking pan, and place the pan in the oven until the butter has melted. Remove the pan from the oven, and tilt it until the butter spreads all over the bottom and 1 inch up the sides of the pan. Break the eggs one by one into the baking pan, and sprinkle with salt and pepper to taste. Bake the eggs for 5 to 7 minutes, or until the whites have cooked into a solid layer. Remove the pan from the oven, and cut the eggs into 12 sections with a knife. Turn the eggs gently with a spatula, and return the pan to the oven for an additional 2 to 4 minutes, depending on if you prefer the eggs well cooked or runny.

3. Place the wrappers on a counter, and place a portion of hash on one side of the wrapper, leaving a 2-inch margin on one side. Place an egg on top of the hash. Tuck the other side over the filling, and then roll the wrappers gently but firmly, beginning with the filled side. Serve immediately.

NOTE: The corned beef hash can be prepared up to 2 days in advance and refrigerated, tightly covered. Reheat in a microwave oven or over low heat.

Vermont Quesadillas

Sharply flavored Cheddar cheese is one of the few savory foods that work with sweets. In the same way that a slice of Cheddar on top of apple pie is appealing, so is this breakfast quesadilla, which combines cheese with sweet spiced apples and salty ham. *Serves 6*

Vegetable oil spray
3 tablespoons unsalted butter
3 Golden Delicious apples, peeled, cored, and thinly sliced
1/4 cup sugar
1/2 teaspoon apple pie spice or 1/4 teaspoon cinnamon and a pinch of nutmeg and allspice

Six 6-inch flour tortillas
1/2 pound thinly sliced honey-baked ham
1 1/2 cups grated Cheddar

1. Preheat the oven to 450°F. Cover a baking sheet with heavy-duty aluminum foil, and spray the foil with vegetable oil spray.

2. Place the butter in a large skillet and melt it over medium heat. Add the apples, and sprinkle them with the sugar and apple pie spice. Cook over medium high heat for 5 to 7 minutes, stirring frequently, or until the apples are soft and slightly browned. Set aside.

3. Arrange the tortillas so that they are half on the baking sheet. Place a layer of ham on the side of the tortilla resting on the baking sheet, and top with a portion of spiced apples. Sprinkle ¼ cup cheese on top of the apples on each tortilla, and then fold the untreated side over the filling. Press gently with the palm of your hand or a spatula to enclose the filling. Space the quesadillas evenly on the baking sheet, and spray the tops with vegetable oil spray.

4. Bake the quesadillas in the preheated oven for 5 minutes. Turn them gently with a spatula, and bake for an additional 5 minutes, or until they are browned. Remove the pan from the oven, and allow them to sit for 2 minutes. Cut each in half, and serve immediately.

NOTE: The apples can be prepared up to 2 days in advance and refrigerated, tightly covered. There is no need to reheat them before assembling and baking the quesadillas.

Southern Egg Wrap

In the South, biscuits with gravy are a breakfast classic. The same ingredients—sausage with gravy made from the pan drippings and scrambled eggs—can be wrapped. *Serves 6*

SUGGESTED WRAPPERS: Eight-inch flour tortillas ◉ Armenian lavash

1 pound bulk pork sausage, crumbled
4 tablespoons (½ stick) unsalted butter, divided
2 tablespoons all-purpose flour
1 cup milk or light cream, heated
Salt and freshly ground black pepper
12 large eggs
⅓ cup sour cream

1. Cook the sausage in a medium skillet, over medium high heat for 3 to 5 minutes, breaking up all lumps with a spoon, or until the sausage is browned and is no longer pink. Remove the sausage from the pan with a slotted spoon, leaving the fat in the pan. Add 1 tablespoon butter to the skillet, and stir to melt. Add the flour, and stir constantly over low heat with a wooden spoon for about 2 minutes, or until the mixture bubbles and is a rich buttery yellow color but not browned.

2. Slowly but steadily pour the hot milk into the pan, whisking over medium heat until it comes to a boil. If the sauce begins to get lumpy as it approaches the boiling point, whisk vigorously and it will smooth out. Reduce the heat to low, return the sausage to the pan, and simmer the sauce over low heat for 3 minutes, stirring occasionally. Season the sauce with salt and pepper to taste, and keep it hot.

3. Whisk the eggs with the sour cream, and salt and pepper to taste. Melt the remaining butter in a large skillet over low heat. Tilt the pan so that the butter coats the bottom and halfway up the sides. Add the eggs, reduce the heat to low, and cover the pan. Cook the eggs for 3 minutes. Using a metal spatula, scrape the cooked eggs into the center of the pan. Re-cover the pan, and allow the eggs to cook until about $3/4$ firm, scraping again after a few minutes. Remove the pan from the heat, and keep it covered to complete cooking the eggs.

4. Place the wrappers on a counter, and spoon a portion of eggs onto one edge, leaving a $1^{1}/_{2}$-inch margin on both sides. Top the eggs with some of the sausage gravy. Tuck the sides around the filling, and then roll the wrappers firmly but gently, beginning with the filled side. Cut in half, and serve immediately.

NOTE: The sausage gravy can be prepared up to 2 days in advance and refrigerated, tightly covered. Reheat over low heat in a saucepan or in a microwave oven.

Springtime Quesadillas

～～

The combination of asparagus and ham reminds me of spring and traditional Easter dinners. The blend of creamy and sharp cheeses gives this easy brunch wrap the flavor of a cream sauce with a fraction of the work. *Serves 6*

Vegetable oil spray or melted butter
Six 8-inch flour tortillas
4 ounces Boursin cheese with garlic and herbs, softened
1 pound honey-baked ham, thinly sliced
6 large hard-cooked eggs, cut into 6 slices each

3 plum tomatoes, cored, seeded, and thinly sliced
12 asparagus spears, cooked and cut into 2-inch pieces
Freshly ground black pepper
1½ cups grated sharp Cheddar or Gruyère

1. Preheat the oven to 450°F. Cover 2 baking sheets with heavy-duty aluminum foil, and spray the foil with vegetable oil or brush it with melted butter.

2. Arrange the tortillas so they are half on the baking sheets, and spread the half on the sheets with the Boursin cheese. Layer the ham on top of the cheese, and continue with layers of egg, tomato, and asparagus. Season with pepper to taste; little, if any, salt should be used due to the saltiness of the ham. Sprinkle Cheddar or Gruyère on top of the asparagus, and fold the untreated side of each tortilla over the filling, pressing with the palm of your hand or a spatula to seal it tightly. Space the quesadillas evenly on the baking sheets, and spray the tops with oil or brush with butter.

3. Bake the quesadillas in the preheated oven for 5 minutes, turn them gently with a spatula, and bake for an additional 4 to 5 minutes, or until browned. Allow them to sit for 3 minutes, then cut each into 2 or 3 wedges, and serve immediately.

NOTE: The quesadillas can be prepared for baking up to 1 day in advance. Refrigerate them on a platter with the layers separated by sheets of plastic wrap or waxed paper. If assembling them in advance, do not spray the tortillas with oil until just prior to baking.

Ham and Fruit Salsa Wraps

These wraps are perfect for a light breakfast. They contrast refreshing fruit salad with sweetened cream cheese, and the ham adds a salty note. For an even lighter dish, omit the ham. *Serves 6*

SUGGESTED WRAPPERS: Eight-inch flour tortillas ◎ pita bread

**One 8-ounce package cream cheese,
  softened**
¼ cup maple syrup
½ cup finely diced fresh pineapple
**½ papaya, peeled, seeded, and finely
  diced**

½ mango, peeled and finely diced
**2 tablespoons raspberry or balsamic
  vinegar**
1 pound thinly sliced baked ham

1. Combine the cream cheese and maple syrup in a small bowl, and beat well. Combine the pineapple, papaya, mango, and vinegar. Stir gently.

2. Place the tortillas on a counter, and spread the cream cheese on the surface of each. Place a few slices of ham over the cream cheese. Using a slotted spoon, place a portion of fruit salsa on one half of each tortilla, leaving a 1½-inch margin on one side. Tuck the side over the filling, and then roll each tortilla firmly but gently, beginning with the filled side. Serve immediately.

NOTE: If using pita bread, spread the cream cheese on both sides of the pocket. Fold a few slices of ham into a shape to fit inside the pita bread, and spoon a portion of fruit salsa into the middle of the ham packet. Tuck the ham packet inside the pita, and serve immediately. The fruit salsa can be made 1 day in advance and refrigerated, tightly covered.

Ricotta and Mixed Berry Calzone

Ricotta cheese, like cream cheese, is incredibly versatile; it can be made savory or sweet, and it adds a creamy texture without excessive richness to dishes. In these cal-zone, sweet ricotta is melded with succulent fresh berries, making it a great way to end a brunch. *Serves 6*

1 pound ricotta cheese
1/3 cup sugar, divided
3 tablespoons Grand Marnier, kirsch, or
    any fruit-flavored liqueur
1 cup sliced strawberries

1 cup raspberries, blackberries, or other
    berries of your choosing
Pizza dough (homemade or purchased
    refrigerated)
Cornmeal

1. Preheat the oven to 450°F. Place a pizza stone or baking sheet in the oven to preheat.

2. Combine the ricotta, 1/4 cup sugar, and Grand Marnier in a mixing bowl, and stir well. Place the berries in another mixing bowl, and sprinkle with the remaining sugar.

3. Divide the pizza dough into 6 parts, and roll each one into a 6-inch circle. Spread a portion of ricotta on half of each circle, leaving a 1/2-inch margin around it. Arrange the berries on top of the cheese, brush the edge of each calzone with water, and fold over the untreated half-circle of dough. Press the edges together with the tines of a fork to seal in the filling. Sprinkle the hot baking sheet or pizza stone with corn-meal, and space the calzone evenly on it.

4. Bake for 10 minutes, then reduce the oven temperature to 400°F., and bake for an additional 10 minutes, or until the crust is browned. Serve immediately.

NOTE Thinly sliced peaches or plums can be used in place of or along with the berries.

Arugula, Bacon, and Egg Salad

Based on an Italian dish, this salad—wrapped for portability—proves that opposites attract. The peppery arugula and sharp vinaigrette are a perfect foil to the creamy eggs and crunchy bacon. For a spring or summer brunch, this delicious combination is filling yet light. *Serves 6*

SUGGESTED WRAPPERS: Pita bread ◎ eight-inch flour tortillas

12 large eggs
1/2 cup light cream or whole milk
Salt and freshly ground black pepper
3 tablespoons unsalted butter
3 cups tightly packed, stemmed, and
   rinsed fresh arugula leaves

1/3 cup vinaigrette salad dressing
1 pound bacon, fried crisp, drained and
   crumbled

1. Whisk the eggs with the cream or milk, and season with salt and pepper to taste. Place the butter in a large skillet, and melt it over medium heat. Tilt the pan so that the butter coats the bottom and halfway up the sides of the pan. Add the eggs, reduce the heat to low, and cover the pan. Cook the eggs for 3 minutes. Using a metal spatula, scrape the cooked eggs into the center of the pan. Re-cover the pan, and allow the eggs to cook until about 3/4 firm, scraping again after a few minutes.

2. While the eggs are cooking, toss the arugula with the salad dressing and bacon in a large mixing bowl. Scrape the hot eggs into the mixing bowl, and toss the eggs with the salad. Spoon the salad into the pita pockets, and serve immediately.

NOTE: If using tortillas, spoon a portion of salad onto one edge, leaving a 1½-inch margin on the sides. Tuck the sides in to enclose the filling, and roll the tortillas firmly but gently, beginning with the filled edge. Cut in half, and serve immediately.

Smoked Salmon and Herbed Cream Cheese Roll Ups

Rather than diluting the luscious taste of smoked salmon with a doughy bagel, these easy roll ups allow the filling to be the star. To serve as an appetizer at a brunch or cocktail party, roll the filling in 10-inch flour tortillas, trim the ends, and cut the rolls into 1-inch sections. *Serves 6*

One 8-ounce package cream cheese, softened
3 scallions, trimmed, white parts and 3 inches of green tops cut into ½-inch pieces
1 teaspoon crushed garlic
¼ cup packed fresh parsley leaves
1 tablespoon freshly squeezed lemon juice

1 tablespoon sour cream
Salt and freshly ground black pepper
Six 6-inch flour tortillas
6 ounces thinly sliced smoked salmon
18 chives, cut into 5-inch lengths
½ medium cucumber, peeled, halved, and seeded

1. Place the cream cheese in a food processor fitted with the steel blade, and process until fluffy. Add the scallions, garlic, parsley, lemon juice, and sour cream. Process with an on-and-off pulsing action until the scallions and parsley are finely chopped. Season with salt and pepper to taste. Scrape the mixture into a bowl, and keep at room temperature.

2. Lay the tortillas out on a counter. Spread a thin layer of the cream cheese mixture on the entire surface of each tortilla, then spread a heavier layer on one half of the tortilla. Place a layer of salmon over half of each tortilla, and lay chives on top of it. Slice each cucumber half lengthwise into 3 long pieces, and place 1 cucumber slice at the bottom of the filled side of each tortilla.

3. Roll the tortillas firmly but gently, beginning with the filled side. Cut in half on the diagonal, and serve immediately.

NOTE: The cream cheese mixture can be prepared 1 day in advance and refrigerated, tightly covered. Allow it to reach room temperature and become softened before assembling the dish.

Garden Vegetable Egg Bake

Since one of my mottos is "I'd rather cook dinner for twenty than breakfast for two," this dish appeals to me because except for the eggs, these wraps can be prepared the night before. The herbed vegetables and creamy cheese add a wonderful flavor to eggs. The garlic is optional, since a few guests to whom I've served this dish don't share my enthusiasm for garlic in the morning. *Serves 6*

SUGGESTED WRAPPERS: Pita bread ◎ eight-inch flour tortillas ◎ Armenian lavash

3 tablespoons vegetable oil
3/4 cup chopped red onion
2 teaspoons minced garlic (optional)
1 red bell pepper, seeds and ribs
    removed, coarsely chopped
1 1/2 cups diced mushrooms

1 teaspoon dried Italian seasoning
One 1-pound can diced tomatoes,
    drained
Salt and freshly ground black pepper
6 large eggs
1 cup grated Monterey Jack

1. Preheat the oven to 350°F. Heat the oil over medium high heat in a large oven-proof skillet. Add the onion and garlic, if used, and sauté for 2 minutes, stirring constantly. Add the red bell pepper and mushrooms, and sauté for 3 minutes. Add the Italian seasoning and tomatoes, and season with salt and pepper to taste. Bring to a boil and cook for 3 minutes, or until the mushrooms are cooked and the sauce has slightly thickened. Turn off the heat.

2. Smooth the surface of the vegetable mixture, and then make 6 indentations, evenly spaced around the pan. Break an egg into each indentation, season the eggs with salt and pepper to taste, and sprinkle cheese over the top of the vegetables.

3. Place the skillet in the preheated oven, and bake for 12 to 15 minutes, or until the eggs are just set. Using a spatula or large spoon, tuck an egg into each pita pocket, and then spoon the vegetables around it. Serve immediately.

NOTE: If using flour tortillas, place an egg on one edge, leaving a 1½-inch margin on one side. Place a portion of vegetables on top of the egg. Tuck in the side, and roll the tortilla firmly but gently, beginning with the filled side. Serve immediately. The vegetable mixture can be made 1 day in advance and refrigerated, tightly covered. Reheat it over low heat in a skillet before adding the eggs.

Stuffed Brunch Peppers

Any vegetable—from lettuce cups to baked potato skins—can become a wrapper as long it can hold a filling firmly. In this case, colorful bell peppers are stuffed with sweet Italian sausage, tomato sauce, and eggs and baked. They make a stunning presentation at a buffet brunch. *Serves 6*

6 bell peppers (any color) that sit evenly when placed on a flat surface
2 tablespoons olive oil
¼ cup Italian-flavored bread crumbs
1 pound bulk sweet Italian sausage or 1 pound link sausage, casings removed, chopped

½ cup spaghetti sauce
6 large eggs
Salt and freshly ground black pepper
3 tablespoons freshly grated Parmesan

1. Cut the tops off the peppers, and discard the tops and seeds. Pull out the ribs with your fingers. Bring a large pot of salted water to a boil, and blanch the peppers for 4 minutes. Remove them from the water with tongs, and drain them upside down on paper towels.

2. Preheat the oven to 375°F. Heat the olive oil in a medium skillet over medium heat. Add the bread crumbs and sauté, stirring constantly, for 3 to 4 minutes, or until they are browned. Scrape the crumbs out of the pan, and set aside.

3. In the same pan, cook the sausage over medium high heat, breaking up lumps with a fork. Sauté the sausage for about 5 minutes, stirring frequently, or until brown and no trace of pink remains. Remove the sausage from the pan with a slotted spoon, and drain on paper towels. Place the sausage in a small mixing bowl, and stir in the spaghetti sauce.

4. Divide the sausage mixture into the bottom of each pepper. Break an egg on top of it, and sprinkle it with salt and pepper to taste. Sprinkle the eggs with the toasted bread crumbs and Parmesan.

5. Bake for 20 minutes, or until the egg whites are set and the yolks are still slightly liquid. Serve immediately.

NOTE: The peppers can be prepared for cooking up to a few hours in advance. Bake them just prior to serving.

Decadent Dessert Wraps

Wrapping even extends to the sweet finale of the meal, and this chapter will add a myriad of options to your list of picnic favorites.

Some desserts, such as turnovers made from pastry dough, have always been wraps, masquerading under another name. For summer picnics, you'll want to pack Fresh Peach Turnovers; in winter, Chocolate Pecan Turnovers flavored with bourbon are wrapped for plate-free enjoyment.

Other recipes transform a flour tortilla from a neutral casing for savory foods to a crisp, cookielike wrapper for sweets. And others are based on fillings traditionally used with other pastry wrappings that have been updated to make them easier, lighter, and faster to wrap and roll—Easy Apple Strudels are an example.

One of my favorite party desserts, a peanut butter and chocolate pie, is transformed in this chapter into Chocolate Peanut Butter Roll Ups that are ready in a matter of minutes when the filling is wrapped in a tortilla.

Candy Bar Quesadillas

~~~~~~

When flour tortillas are sprinkled with sugar before baking, they become like crispy, light cookies. This wrap works well with any sort of candy bar. My favorite is Snickers, but I've also made these with Almond Joys and a chocolate bar with nuts. The result is a blending of creamy cheese and crisp cookie with the candy of your choosing. *Serves 6*

Six 6-inch flour tortillas
One 8-ounce package cream cheese,
    softened
Two to three 2-ounce candy bars, each
    cut into 15 thin slices

Vegetable oil spray or melted butter
4 tablespoons sugar

1. Preheat the oven to 450°F. Cover a baking sheet with heavy-duty aluminum foil, and spray the foil with oil or brush it with melted butter.

2. Place the tortillas so they are half on the baking sheet, and spread equal amounts of cream cheese over half of each circle. Top with slices of candy. Press the quesadillas together gently into half-circles, and space them evenly on the baking sheet. Spray the tops with vegetable oil spray, and sprinkle with sugar.

3. Bake the quesadillas in the preheated oven for 5 minutes. Turn the quesadillas gently with a spatula, spray and sprinkle the other side with sugar. Bake for an additional 3 to 4 minutes, or until the quesadillas are browned. Remove the pan from the oven, allow the quesadillas to sit for 2 minutes, then cut each in half, and serve immediately.

NOTE: The quesadillas can be prepared up to a few hours in advance and kept at room temperature.

Creamy Quesadillas with Minted Fruit

There are endless variations to this luscious dessert wrap; feel free to experiment with what fruits are ripe in your kitchen or market. In place of the fruits listed, choose fresh diced or sliced fruits that cook quickly, such as any type of berry, and other fruits such as bananas, orange sections, plums, or nectarines. *Serves 6*

Vegetable oil spray or melted butter
One 8-ounce package cream cheese, softened
2 tablespoons kirsch, Grand Marnier, or any fruit-flavored liqueur
1 teaspoon grated orange zest
1/2 cup diced strawberries

1/2 cup diced fresh mango or papaya
1/2 cup halved green or red seedless grapes
2 tablespoons chopped fresh mint
Six 6-inch flour tortillas
1/4 cup sugar

1. Preheat the oven to 450°F. Cover a baking sheet with heavy-duty aluminum foil, and spray the foil with oil or brush it with melted butter.

2. Combine the cream cheese, kirsch, and orange zest in a mixing bowl, and beat well. Place the strawberries, mango, grapes, and mint in a mixing bowl, and toss to combine.

3. Lay the tortillas on the counter, and spread the entire surface of each with the cream cheese mixture. Arrange a portion of fruit on one half of each tortilla, and fold the other half over the fruit. With the palm of your hand or a spatula, gently press the tortillas closed. Space the quesadillas evenly on the baking sheet, and spray the tops with oil or brush them with melted butter. Sprinkle the tops with sugar.

4. Bake the quesadillas in the preheated oven for 5 minutes. Turn them gently with a spatula, sprinkle the other side with sugar, and bake for an additional 3 to 5 minutes, or until browned. Allow them to sit for 3 minutes, then cut each in half, and serve immediately.

Caramel Apple Quesadillas

When you have a hankering for apple pie, here are the same flavors all wrapped up in just minutes. *Serves 6*

Vegetable oil spray or melted butter
18 caramel candies, unwrapped
2 tablespoons milk
¼ teaspoon cinnamon

Six 6-inch flour tortillas, softened
2 Golden Delicious apples, peeled and
     thinly sliced
3 tablespoons sugar

1. Preheat the oven to 375°F. Cover a baking sheet with heavy-duty aluminum foil, and spray the foil with oil or brush it with melted butter.

2. Place the caramel candies and milk in a small microwave-safe bowl, and microwave at MEDIUM (50%) for 45 seconds. Stir, and repeat as necessary until the caramel is smooth. Stir in the cinnamon.

3. Spread the caramel mixture on each tortilla to about ½ inch from the edge. Arrange apple slices over one half of each tortilla, and fold over the other half. Press down with the palm of your hand or with a spatula to enclose the filling.

4. Space the quesadillas evenly on the baking sheet, spray with oil or brush with butter, and then sprinkle with half the sugar. Bake for 10 minutes, then turn them with a spatula, sprinkle with the remaining sugar, and bake for an additional 10 minutes, or until the quesadillas are browned. Allow to sit for 3 minutes, then cut each into halves and serve immediately.

Ice Cream Sundae Burritos

What combination of ingredients comprises the perfect ice cream sundae is a matter of personal preference, so here's a general procedure for how to create a hand-holdable sundae. Ice cream, sauce, and toppings are all included. *Serves 6*

Six 10-inch flour tortillas
1¹/₂ cups thick ice cream sauce or fruit jam
1 cup sundae toppings such as chopped nuts, sliced fruit, broken-up candy bars, or cookie crumbs

1¹/₂ pints ice cream (any flavor of your choosing)
Vegetable oil spray or melted butter
6 tablespoons sugar

1. Spread the tortillas on a counter, and spread ¹/₄ cup sauce in the center of each tortilla. Using scissors, cut away the cartons from the ice cream, and then cut the ice cream vertically into six pieces. Place one ice cream quarter on top of the sauce in the tortilla, and sprinkle with any additional ingredients desired.

2. Fold the ends of the tortilla over the filling, and then roll the burrito. Place the burritos in the freezer for a minimum of 1 hour, or until very hard.

3. Just prior to serving, turn on the oven broiler. Preheat only until the broiling element is glowing and hot. Line a broiler pan with heavy-duty aluminum foil, and place the burritos on top of the foil. Spray with vegetable oil spray or brush with melted butter. Sprinkle ¹/₂ tablespoon sugar on top of each burrito, and place the pan 6 inches from the broiling element. Broil for 1 to 1¹/₂ minutes, or until the sugar is lightly browned. Gently turn the burritos with tongs, spray or brush with oil or melted butter, and sprinkle with the remaining sugar. Broil until browned on the other side. Serve immediately.

NOTE: The burritos can be frozen for up to 3 days before broiling.

Chocolate Peanut Butter Roll Ups

Wrap up creamy peanut butter mousse and dense chocolate ganache in flour tortillas for a homemade Reese's wrap. While you have to start this dish about an hour in advance to allow the peanut butter mousse to chill, the actual preparation time is just minutes. *Serves 6*

½ cup creamy peanut butter
⅓ cup sugar
One 3-ounce package cream cheese
½ teaspoon vanilla extract
⅔ cup heavy cream, divided
¼ pound good-quality bittersweet or semisweet chocolate, finely chopped

Six 8-inch flour tortillas
4 tablespoons (½ stick) unsalted butter, melted
¼ cup sugar
¼ cup unsweetened cocoa powder

1. In the bowl of an electric mixer, cream the peanut butter and sugar until light and fluffy at medium speed. Add the cream cheese and vanilla, and beat well. Whip ⅓ cup heavy cream until medium-soft peaks form, and fold the cream into the peanut butter mixture until thoroughly combined. Refrigerate for 30 minutes, or until slightly firm.

2. While the mousse is chilling, place the chopped chocolate in a small mixing bowl. Bring the remaining ⅓ cup cream to a boil in a small saucepan or in a glass measuring cup in a microwave oven at 100% (HIGH), and pour it over the chocolate. Stir until melted and thoroughly combined. Set mixture aside until it is firm enough to spread; it should have the consistency of cream cheese.

3. Remove the mousse from the refrigerator. Beat on the lowest speed of the mixer for at least 5 minutes, preferably longer, until mousse is light and fluffy.

4. Preheat the oven broiler. Cover a baking sheet with heavy-duty aluminum foil. Place the tortillas on a counter, and spread a thick layer of chocolate 3 inches wide in the center of each tortilla, leaving a 1½-inch margin on both sides. Place a portion of mousse at the bottom of each tortilla, below the chocolate. Tuck the sides in to enclose the filling, and gently roll the tortillas into a cylinder. Place the tortillas, seam side down, on the baking sheet. Brush the rolls with melted butter. Combine the sugar and cocoa powder, and sprinkle the mixture heavily over the rolls.

5. Broil the rolls 6 inches from the broiler unit for 1 to 2 minutes, or until the sugar on the top has melted. Remove the pan from the broiler, and serve immediately.

NOTE: The peanut butter and chocolate mixtures can be prepared up to 1 day in advance and refrigerated, tightly covered. Allow the chocolate to reach a spreadable consistency before assembling the dessert. Or the rolls can be prepared for final broiling up to 2 hours in advance and refrigerated.

Very Berry Burritos

These burritos are similar to indulging in rich cheesecake topped with vivid fresh fruit. The berries are like a fruit salad, since they retain texture, and their flavor is boosted with jam and liqueur. *Serves 6*

½ cup raspberry jam
2 tablespoons crème de cassis
1 pint fresh blueberries, rinsed and
    picked over
1 pint fresh strawberries, rinsed,
    stemmed, and sliced
One 8-ounce package cream cheese,
    softened

⅓ cup confectioners' sugar
1 teaspoon grated lemon zest
1 teaspoon grated orange zest
Six 8-inch flour tortillas
3 tablespoons melted butter
¼ cup granulated sugar

1. Preheat the oven broiler. Cover 1 baking sheet with heavy-duty aluminum foil.

2. Combine the jam and crème de cassis in a large mixing bowl, whisking until smooth. Add the blueberries and strawberries to the bowl, and toss gently to coat evenly. In separate bowl, beat the cream cheese with confectioners' sugar, lemon zest, and orange zest until light and fluffy.

3. Spread some of the cheese mixture on one side of each tortilla, leaving a 1½-inch margin on both sides. Place a portion of berries on top of the cheese, and dot the top of the berries with more cheese.

4. Tuck the sides of the tortillas around the filling, and then roll the tortillas firmly but gently. Place the tortilla rolls, seam side down, on the baking sheet. Brush the rolls with melted butter, and sprinkle them with granulated sugar. Place the baking sheet 8 inches from the broiler element, and broil for 1 to 2 minutes, or until the rolls are lightly browned. Turn gently with tongs, and sprinkle the other side with sugar. Broil for 1 to 2 minutes, then remove the burritos from the oven, and serve immediately.

NOTE: Any combination of berries can be used for this dessert, and the choice of jam and liqueur can also be varied.

Substituting Chocolate

Need semisweet chocolate for a recipe, but only have unsweetened chocolate on hand? Combine 4 teaspoons sugar per 1 ounce unsweetened chocolate. Also, 3 tablespoons cocoa powder plus 1 tablespoon vegetable shortening equals 1 ounce unsweetened chocolate.

Fresh Peach Turnovers

Summer is fresh peach season, but who wants to spend time making peach pies? Peach turnovers prepared with refrigerated pie crust are quick-and-easy wraps. While sweet fresh peaches need little to create perfection, I like the color and flavor contrast provided by the tart dried cherries, but you can omit them. *Serves 6*

¹/₄ cup dried cherries
2 to 3 fresh ripe peaches, depending on size, peeled and stoned
1 tablespoon all-purpose flour
¹/₃ cup sugar
Pinch of cinnamon

1 package refrigerated pie-crust sheets, at room temperature (or enough homemade dough for a double-crust pie)
1 large egg, lightly beaten

1. Preheat the oven to 400°F. Cover a baking sheet with heavy-duty aluminum foil.

2. Place the dried cherries in a small saucepan with ¹/₂ cup water, and bring to a boil. Remove the pan from the heat, and allow the cherries to rehydrate for 10 minutes. Cut the peaches into ¹/₂-inch pieces, and place them in a mixing bowl. Drain the cherries, and add them to the peaches. Mix the flour, sugar, and cinnamon, and sprinkle the mixture over the fruit. Stir well to combine.

3. Place 1 pie-crust sheet between 2 sheets of plastic wrap, and roll it into a 12-inch circle. Using a dish or pot lid as a guide, cut three 6-inch circles from the pie-crust sheet. Repeat with the second sheet. Place a portion of filling on one side of each circle, leaving a ¹/₂-inch border. Fold the dough over the filling, and crimp the edges of the turnovers with the tines of a fork. Cut four ¹/₂-inch slits in the top of each turnover, and brush the tops with beaten egg. Space the turnovers evenly on the baking sheet.

4. Bake the turnovers in the center of the preheated oven for 35 to 40 minutes, or until golden brown. Allow to sit for 5 minutes before serving; they can also be served at room temperature.

NOTE: Dried cranberries can be used in place of the dried cherries.

Chocolate Logs

The combination of chocolate, nuts, and cream cheese is a perennial favorite. These easy roll ups contain the same ingredients as a cream cheese brownie, but they need no baking and can be ready in just minutes. The filling is enclosed in slices of flattened white bread, and then coated with more cheese dusted with cocoa. *Serves 6*

Two 3-ounce packages cream cheese,
    softened
2/3 cup confectioners' sugar, divided
1/2 teaspoon vanilla extract
1/2 cup chopped good-quality
    bittersweet or semisweet chocolate

1/2 cup chopped walnuts or pecans,
    toasted
One 1-pound loaf white bread, crusts
    trimmed and rolled flat (page 9)
1/4 cup cocoa powder
1 tablespoon heavy cream or milk

1. Combine the cream cheese, 1/3 cup sugar, and vanilla in a bowl, and beat well. Reserve 1/3 of the mixture, and stir in the chocolate and nuts into the remaining 2/3.

2. Place 1 heaping tablespoon of the mixture along the center of the long side of each slice of bread. Bring the sides of the bread up to enclose the filling, and place the rolls, seam side down, on a baking sheet covered with plastic wrap. Repeat with remaining filling and bread slices.

3. Mix the remaining sugar and the cocoa together in a small bowl. Stir the cream into the remaining cheese mixture, and spread this on the tops and sides of the rolls. Sift the cocoa mixture over the cheese. Cut rolls in half using a sharp serrated knife, if desired, and serve immediately.

NOTE: The rolls can be prepared up to step 3, then refrigerated, tightly covered. Complete assembly just prior to serving.

Bananas Foster Roll Ups

Bananas Foster, silky hot bananas sautéed in spiced and spiked butter and served atop ice cream, was invented at the legendary Brennan's in New Orleans, where it is prepared tableside. These roll ups in delicate rice paper pancakes capture the same flavor and texture contrasts in a hand-holdable form. *Serves 6*

1 pint vanilla ice cream
1/3 cup firmly packed dark brown sugar
1/2 teaspoon ground cinnamon
2 tablespoons unsalted butter
2 ripe bananas

1 tablespoon light rum
2 tablespoons banana liqueur
1/2 cup granulated sugar
24 rice paper pancakes

   1. Cut away the carton from the pint of ice cream. Cut the ice cream in half horizontally, and then cut each half into 6 logs. Place the ice cream logs on a baking sheet lined with plastic wrap, and freeze until solid. Keep frozen until ready to serve.
   2. Place the brown sugar, cinnamon, and butter in medium skillet. Cook over medium heat until the sugar has melted. Peel the bananas, slice them lengthwise, and then cut each section into thirds.
   3. Add the banana pieces to the sugar mixture. Cook for 2 minutes over medium heat, or until the bananas begin to soften. Add the rum and liqueur, and cook for 2 minutes longer. Allow to cool to room temperature.
   4. Place the granulated sugar in a large mixing bowl. Add 6 cups of very hot tap water, and stir to dissolve the sugar. Place the rice paper pancakes on a dish, and keep them covered with a damp tea towel. Place a damp tea towel in front of you on the counter. Immerse 1 pancake in the hot water for 3 seconds. Remove it, gently shaking off moisture. Place it on the towel, and place 1 ice cream log 2 inches from one edge, leaving a 1 1/2-inch margin on both sides. Top the ice cream with a banana section and some of the sauce. Tuck the sides of the pancake over the filling, and then tuck the

lower edge over the filling. Roll the pancake firmly but gently. Soak another pancake, and place the rolled one in the center. Fold the sides over the roll, and wrap the second pancake on top of the first. Repeat with remaining pancakes, and serve immediately.

NOTE: The banana mixture can be prepared up to 1 day in advance and refrigerated, tightly covered. Allow it to reach room temperature before rolling and filling the pancakes.

Pineapple, Macadamia, and Coconut Turnovers

The combination of crunchy and sweet macadamia nuts with toasted coconut and succulent pineapple is as sensuous as a tropical Hawaiian breeze. These flavors are especially good at the end of an Asian-inspired meal. *Serves 6*

One 3-ounce package cream cheese, softened
$^1/_3$ cup pineapple jam
2 tablespoons rum
$^1/_2$ teaspoon vanilla extract
1 cup macadamia nuts, coarsely chopped

$^1/_2$ cup sweetened grated coconut, lightly toasted
$^1/_4$ cup chopped fresh pineapple
1 package refrigerated pie-crust sheets, at room temperature (or enough for a double crust pie)
1 large egg, lightly beaten

1. Preheat the oven to 400°F. Cover a baking sheet with heavy-duty aluminum foil.
2. Combine the cream cheese, pineapple jam, rum, and vanilla in a mixing bowl, and beat well. Fold in the macadamia nuts, coconut, and pineapple.

3. Place 1 pie-crust sheet between 2 sheets of plastic wrap, and roll it into a 12-inch circle. Using a dish or pot lid as a guide, cut three 6-inch circles from the pie-crust sheet. Repeat with the second sheet. Place a portion of filling on one side of each circle, leaving a 1/2-inch border. Fold the dough over the filling, and crimp the edges of the turnovers with the tines of a fork. Cut four 1/2-inch slits in the top of each turnover, and brush the tops with beaten egg. Space the turnovers evenly on the baking sheet.

4. Bake the turnovers in the center of the preheated oven for 35 to 40 minutes, or until golden brown. Allow to sit for 5 minutes before serving; they can also be served at room temperature.

NOTE: The turnovers can be prepared for baking 1 day in advance and refrigerated, covered with plastic wrap. Brush them with beaten egg just prior to baking.

Chocolate Pecan Turnovers

~~~~~

Imagine the most sinfully rich chocolate pecan pie, and this easy dessert wrap tops it. Chocolate chips, caramel candy squares, and crunchy pecans are piled into rounds of ready-made pie crust and baked. *Serves 6*

24 caramel candies, unwrapped
1/2 cup heavy cream
1/4 cup bourbon or rum (optional)
8 ounces chopped pecans, toasted
One 6-ounce package semisweet chocolate chips

1 package refrigerated pie-crust sheets, at room temperature (or enough homemade dough for a double-crust pie)
1 large egg, lightly beaten

1. Preheat the oven to 400°F. Cover a baking sheet with heavy-duty aluminum foil.

2. Place the candies and cream in a large microwave-safe bowl or in a medium saucepan. Microwave at MEDIUM (50%) for 1 minute. Stir and repeat as necessary until the mixture is melted and smooth. Alternately, cook over low heat, stirring frequently, until melted and smooth. Add the bourbon, if used, and stir until smooth. Allow to cool for 10 minutes. Add the nuts and chocolate chips to the caramel mixture, and stir gently to combine.

3. Place 1 pie-crust sheet between 2 sheets of plastic wrap, and roll it into a 12-inch circle. Using a dish or pot lid as a guide, cut three 6-inch circles from the pie-crust sheet. Repeat with the second sheet. Place a portion of filling on one side of each circle, leaving a 1/2-inch border. Fold the dough over the filling, and crimp the edges of the turnovers with the tines of a fork. Cut four 1/2-inch slits in the top of each turnover, and brush the tops with beaten egg. Space the turnovers evenly on the baking sheet.

4. Bake the turnovers in the center of the preheated oven for 35 to 40 minutes, or until golden brown. Allow to sit for 5 minutes before serving; they can also be served at room temperature.

NOTE: The turnovers can be prepared for baking 1 day in advance and refrigerated, covered with plastic wrap. Brush them with beaten egg just prior to baking.

Chips vs. Bits

Chocolate chips and bits of broken chocolate should not be substituted for one another. Chocolate chips, which are formulated to retain their shape at high heat, react differently in baking than chopped chocolate, and can form gritty granules in a cooled dessert.

Easy Apple Strudels

Apples with cinnamon and raisins wrapped in layers of crisp strudel dough have long been a favorite dessert, but delicate phyllo dough is difficult to work with and requires frequent brushings of melted butter to keep it moist. Rice paper pancakes create little "cigars" of strudel and yield the same taste sensation. Since these are small, I make 2 per person. *Serves 6*

1/3 cup raisins

1/4 cup brandy, or 1/4 cup water mixed
    with 1/4 teaspoon rum flavoring

2 Granny Smith apples, peeled, cored,
    and cut into 1/2-inch dice

2 tablespoons freshly squeezed lemon
    juice

1/4 cup firmly packed dark brown sugar

1/2 teaspoon apple pie spice

1/3 cup chopped walnuts, toasted

5 tablespoons melted unsalted butter,
    divided

1/2 cup granulated sugar

12 rice paper pancakes

   1. Combine the raisins and brandy in a small bowl. Marinate for 30 minutes, or longer if the raisins are hard.

   2. Toss the apples with the lemon juice to prevent discoloration. Add the brown sugar, apple pie spice, nuts, raisins, and 1 tablespoon melted butter. Toss to combine.

   3. Preheat the oven to 425°F. Cover 1 baking sheet with heavy-duty aluminum foil. Place 6 cups of very hot tap water in a mixing bowl, and stir in the granulated sugar until dissolved.

   4. Place the rice paper pancakes on a large plate, and keep them covered with a damp tea towel. Place a damp tea towel on the counter in front of you. Immerse 1 pancake into the hot water for 3 seconds, and then place it on the damp towel; it will become pliable in a few seconds. Brush the pancake with melted butter. Place 1/4 cup apple filling in a log shape on one side of the pancake, leaving a 1-inch border. Tuck the ends over the filling, and then roll the pancake firmly. Place it, seam side down, on the baking sheet, and brush the top with melted butter. Repeat with the remaining pancakes.

5. Bake for 20 minutes in the preheated oven, or until the rolls are crisp and brown. Serve hot or at room temperature.

NOTE: The rolls can be prepared for baking up to 2 hours in advance. Any dried fruit—such as cherries or chopped dried apricots—can be used instead of raisins.

Dried Fruit Calzone

〜〜〜

Dried fruits are more intensely flavored than their fresh counterparts since most of the water has been dehydrated as a method of preservation. When this combination of fruits is cooked briefly with flavorings, it becomes similar to a thick jam. This easy filling is then wrapped in pizza dough. These are a wonderful winter dessert, and an excellent addition to a holiday party table since they are hand-holdable. *Serves 6*

¹/₂ cup chopped dried apricots
¹/₂ cup golden or dark raisins
¹/₂ cup chopped dried figs
¹/₄ cup dried currants
¹/₄ cup chopped dried apples
¹/₄ cup firmly packed dark brown sugar
¹/₂ cup freshly squeezed orange juice
Pinch of salt

2 tablespoons unsalted butter
2 teaspoons grated lemon zest
3 tablespoons brandy, rum, or more
   orange juice
1 recipe pizza dough (homemade or
   purchased refrigerated)
Cornmeal

1. Combine the apricots, raisins, figs, currants, apples, brown sugar, orange juice, and salt in a medium saucepan. Bring the mixture to a boil over medium heat, and cook, stirring frequently, for 10 minutes, or until the mixture thickens. Remove the pan from the heat, and stir in the butter, lemon zest, and brandy, if used. Scrape the mixture into a shallow bowl, and after 10 minutes at room temperature, refrigerate it for 20 minutes before assembling the calzone.

2. While the fruit filling is chilling, preheat the oven to 450°F. Place a pizza stone or baking sheet in the oven to preheat.

3. Divide the pizza dough into 6 parts, and roll each one into a 6-inch circle. Place a portion of fruit on half of each circle, leaving a ½-inch margin around it. Brush the edge of the calzone with water, and fold over the untreated dough. Press the edges together with the tines of a fork to seal in the filling. Sprinkle the hot baking sheet or pizza stone with cornmeal, and space the calzone evenly.

4. Bake for 10 minutes, then reduce the oven temperature to 400°F. and bake for an additional 10 minutes, or until the crust is browned. Serve immediately.

NOTE: The fruit mixture can be prepared 3 days in advance and refrigerated, tightly covered.

To Soften Raisins

If raisins have become as hard as pellets, soak them in hot tap water for 15 minutes, place them in a steamer over boiling water and steam for 5 minutes, or poach them in a small amount of liquid for 5 minutes.

Index